Buildi...
Agreem...

ROGER FISHER teaches negotiation at Harvard Law School, where he is Williston Professor of Law *Emeritus* and Director of the Harvard Negotiation Project. He has spent the past forty years studying, writing, and teaching about negotiation. He developed the concept of interest-based negotiation and has consulted on differences ranging from business disputes to international conflicts. He advised the Iranian and United States governments in their negotiations for the release of the American diplomats being held hostage in Tehran. He helped to design the process used by President Carter in the successful Camp David negotiations between President Sadat of Egypt and Prime Minister Begin of Israel. In South Africa, he trained the white Cabinet and the African National Congress Negotiating Committee prior to the constitutional talks that led to the end of apartheid. He advised three of the five Central American countries on a regional peace plan in advance of the Esquipulas II treaty, and he worked with the president of Ecuador on a negotiation process that helped to end a long-standing border dispute between Ecuador and Peru. He continues his active interest in working on issues of this kind.

DANIEL SHAPIRO, Associate Director of the Harvard Negotiation Project, is on the faculty at Harvard Law School and in the psychiatry department at Harvard Medical School/McLean Hospital. He holds a doctorate in clinical psychology and specializes in the psychology of negotiation. He directs the International Negotiation Initiative, a Harvard-based project that develops psychologically focused strategies to reduce ethnopolitical violence. He has been on the faculty at the Sloan School of Management, Massachusetts Institute of Technology, and teaches negotiation to corporate executives and diplomats. He has extensive international experience, including training Serbian members of Parliament, Mideast negotiators, Macedonian politicians, and senior U.S. officials. During the Bosnian war, he conducted conflict management trainings in Croatia and Serbia. Through funding from the Soros Foundation, he developed a conflict management program that now reaches nearly one million people across twenty-five countries.

- For additional information on *Building Agreement* (published in the U.S. as *Beyond Reason*) visit our web site at www.beyond-reason.net.

- To contact the authors with questions, comments, and inquiries about lectures or consultation, please e-mail us at rogeranddan@beyond-reason.net.

- To learn more about the Harvard Negotiation Project, visit www.pon.harvard.edu/hnp.

Building Agreement

Using Emotions as You Negotiate

Roger Fisher
and
Daniel Shapiro

BUSINESS
BOOKS

Published by Random House Business Books in 2007

6 8 10 9 7 5

First published in the United States in 2005 by Viking,
an imprint of The Penguin Group, with the title *Beyond Reason*

Random House Business Books
Random House, 20 Vauxhall Bridge Road,
London SW1V 2SA

www.randomhouse.co.uk

Addresses for companies within The Random House Group Limited can be found at:
www.randomhouse.co.uk/offices.htm

The Random House Group Limited Reg. No. 954009

A CIP catalogue record for this book
is available from the British Library

ISBN 9781905211081

The Random House Group Limited supports The Forest Stewardship
Council (FSC®), the leading international forest certification organisation.
Our books carrying the FSC label are printed on FSC® certified paper.
FSC is the only forest certification scheme endorsed by the leading
environmental organisations, including Greenpeace. Our
paper procurement policy can be found at
www.randomhouse.co.uk/environment

Printed and bound in Great Britain by Clays Ltd, St Ives PLC

To Carrie and Mia

WITH MUCH LOVE

(and other positive emotions)

Contents

Introduction

We cannot stop having emotions
any more than we can stop having thoughts.
The challenge is learning to stimulate helpful emotions
in those with whom we negotiate—and in ourselves.

You negotiate every day, whether about where to go for dinner, how much to pay for a secondhand bicycle, or when to terminate an employee. And you have emotions all the time. These may be positive emotions like joy or contentment, or negative emotions like anger, frustration, and guilt.

When you negotiate with others, how should you deal with these emotions—both theirs and yours? As hard as you might try to ignore emotions, they won't go away. They can be distracting, painful, or the cause of a failed agreement. They can divert your attention from an important issue that ought to be resolved now. And yet as you negotiate formally or informally, you have too much to think about to study every emotion that you and others may be feeling and to decide what to do about it. It is hard to manage the very emotions that affect you.

Building Agreement offers a way to deal with this problem. You will learn a strategy to generate positive emotions and to deal with negative ones. No longer will you be at the mercy of your own emotions or those of others. Your negotiations will be more comfortable and more effective. This strategy is powerful enough to use in your toughest negotiations—whether with a difficult colleague, a hard bargainer, or your spouse.

Because *Building Agreement* is about emotions, we (Roger and Dan) have added a personal dimension to our writing. We have included a number of examples drawn from our personal lives as well as from our involvement for many years in the field of negotiation. We each have developed negotiation theory and have trained people from all walks of life, from Mideast negotiators to marital couples, business executives to university students.

This book is a product of our personal learning and research. It builds upon *Getting to YES: Negotiating Agreement Without Giving In*, which is coauthored by Roger and has become a foundation for the widely used process of *interest-based negotiation*. This process suggests that negotiators obtain the best results by understanding each other's interests and working together to produce an agreement that will meet those interests as best they can. (See Seven Elements of Negotiation on page 207 for details.) Many have commented that though the advice in *Getting to YES* is powerful, it does not spend much time addressing the question of how to handle the emotions and relationship issues in our toughest negotiations. This is our attempt to dig into those questions.

This book would not have happened were it not for the late professor Jerome D. Frank, who introduced the two of us. His intuition suggested to him that there might be synergy between "a negotiator interested in psychology" and "a psychologist interested in negotiation." He was right, and we are indebted.

We have worked together for the past five years on this book. It has taken far longer than either of us would have predicted, in part because we have so enjoyed spending time talking together and learning from each other. We now understand far more about emotions in negotiation than the sum total of our combined knowledge a few years back.

In this book, we share some of the excitement of these ideas with you, the reader.

I

The Big Picture

CHAPTER 1

Emotions Are Powerful, Always Present, and Hard to Handle

A prospective customer threatens to back out of an agreement just before the final document is signed. The dealer who sold you a brand new car says that engine problems are not covered under warranty. Your eleven-year-old announces there is simply no way she is going to wear a coat to school on this frigid February morning.

At moments like these, when your blood pressure is rising or anxiety is creeping in, rational advice about how to negotiate seems irrelevant. As constructive and reasonable as you might like to be, you may find yourself saying things like:

"Don't do this to me. If you walk away from this agreement, I'm out of a job."

"What kind of sleazy operation is this? Fix the engine or we'll see you in court."

"Young lady, you're wearing a coat whether you like it or not. Put it on!"

Or perhaps you do not express your emotions in the moment, but let them eat away at you for the rest of the day. If your boss asks you to work all weekend to finish something she didn't get to, do you say okay, but spend the weekend fuming while you consider quitting? Whether you speak up or not, your emotions may take over. You may act in ways that jeopardize reaching agreement, that damage a relationship, or that cost you a lot.

Negotiation involves both your head and your gut—both reason and emotion. In this book, we offer advice to deal with emotions. Negotiation is more than rational argument. Human beings are not computers. In addition to your substantive interests, *you* are a part of the negotiation. Your emotions are there, and they will be involved. So, too, will the emotions of others.

WHAT IS AN EMOTION?

Psychologists Fehr and Russell note that "everyone knows what an emotion is, until asked to give a definition. Then, it seems, no one knows." As we use the term, an emotion is a felt experience. You *feel* an emotion; you don't just think it. When someone says or does something that is personally significant to you, your emotions respond, usually along with associated thoughts, physiological changes, and a desire to *do* something. If a junior colleague tells you to take notes in a meeting, you might feel angry and think, "Who is *he* to tell me what to do?" Your physiology changes as your blood pressure rises, and you feel a desire to insult him.

Emotions can be positive or negative. A positive emotion feels personally uplifting. Whether pride, hope, or relief, a positive emotion feels good. In a negotiation, a positive emotion toward the other person is likely to build *rapport*, a relationship marked by goodwill, understanding, and a feeling of being "in sync." In contrast, anger, frustration, and other negative emotions feel personally distressing, and they are less likely to build rapport.*

---

*As a general negotiating strategy, positive emotions are more likely than negative emotions to foster rapport and collaboration. Yet, tactically, even the negative emotion of anger can enable two people to clear the air and get back together. And, to be sure, sometimes negative feelings such as grief can bring people together as they share the grief.

This book focuses on how you can use positive emotions to help reach a wise agreement. In this chapter, we describe major obstacles you might face as you deal with emotions—both yours and those of others. Subsequent chapters give you a practical framework to overcome these obstacles. The framework does not require you to reveal your deepest emotions or to manipulate others. Instead, it provides you with practical ideas to deal with emotions. You can begin to use the framework immediately.

EMOTIONS CAN BE OBSTACLES TO NEGOTIATION

None of us is spared the reality of emotions. They can ruin any possibility of a wise agreement. They can turn an amicable relationship into a long-lasting feud where everybody gets hurt. And they can sour hopes for a fair settlement. What makes emotions so troubling?

They can divert attention from substantive matters. If you or the other person gets upset, each of you will have to deal with the hassle of emotions. Should you storm out of the room? Apologize? Sit quietly and fume? Your attention shifts from reaching a satisfying agreement to protecting yourself or attacking the other.

They can damage a relationship. Unbridled emotions may be desirable when falling in love. But in a negotiation, they reduce your ability to act wisely. Strong emotions can overshadow your thinking, leaving you at risk of damaging your relationship. In anger, you may interrupt the long-winded comments of a colleague who was just about to suggest an agreement workable for both of you. And in resentment, he may retaliate by remaining silent the next time you need his support.

They can be used to exploit you. If you flinch at another negotiator's proposal or hesitate before telling them* your interests, these observable reactions offer clues about your "true" concerns and

---

*In this book, we sometimes use the third person plural—they, them, or their—where strict grammar would suggest using a singular, such as he or she. Other options seem to lead to some sort of stereotyping or distracting language.

vulnerabilities. Careful observers of your emotional reaction may learn how much you value proposals, issues, and your relationship with them. They may use that information to exploit you.

If those are possible results of emotions, it is not surprising that a negotiator is often advised to avoid them altogether.

EMOTIONS CAN BE A GREAT ASSET

Although emotions are often thought of as obstacles to a negotiation—and certainly can be—they can also be a great asset. They can help us achieve our negotiating purpose, whether to find creative ways to satisfy interests or to improve a rocky relationship.

President Carter used the power of emotions during the historic peace negotiations between Israel and Egypt. He invited Israel's Prime Minister, Menachim Begin, and Egypt's President, Anwar Sadat, to Camp David. His goal was to help the two leaders negotiate a peace agreement. After thirteen long days, the negotiation process was breaking down. The Israelis saw little prospect for reaching agreement.

By this time, Carter had invested a lot of time and energy in the peace process. He could easily have expressed frustration, perhaps approaching Begin with a warning to accept his latest proposal "or else." But an adversarial approach might have caused Begin to abandon the negotiation process completely. It would also have risked damaging the personal relationship between the two leaders.

Instead, Carter made a gesture that had a significant emotional impact. Begin had asked for autographed pictures of Carter, Sadat, and himself to give to his grandchildren. Carter personalized each picture with the name of a Begin grandchild. During the stalemate in talks, Carter handed Begin the photographs. Begin saw his granddaughter's name on the top photograph and spoke her name aloud. His lips trembled. He shuffled through the photographs and said each grandchild's name. He and Carter talked quietly about grandchildren and about war. This was a turning point in the negotiation. Later that day, Begin, Sadat, and Carter signed the Camp David Accord.

The open discussion between Carter and Begin could not have happened if there were a poor relationship between them. Begin talked to Carter about difficult issues without resisting or walking out. The groundwork of positive emotions allowed nonthreatening conversation about serious differences.

This groundwork did not just "happen." It took work. Honest work. Carter and Begin began to establish rapport at their first meeting more than a year prior to the negotiation. They met at the White House, where Carter invited the Prime Minister for an open, private discussion about the Mideast conflict. Months later, Carter and his wife invited Begin and his wife to a private dinner, where they talked about their personal lives, including the murder of Begin's parents and his only brother in the Holocaust. Later, during the Camp David negotiation, Carter demonstrated that he was looking out for each party's welfare. For example, before Begin met with Sadat for the first time at Camp David, Carter alerted Begin that Sadat would present an aggressive proposal; he cautioned Begin not to overreact.

Carter did not want the negotiation to fail, nor did Begin or Sadat. Everyone had an interest in "winning." And positive emotions between Carter and each leader helped to move the negotiation forward.

In an international or everyday negotiation, positive emotions can be essential. They can benefit you in three important ways.

Positive emotions can make it easier to meet substantive interests. Positive emotions toward the other person reduce fear and suspicion, changing your relationship from adversaries to colleagues. As you work side by side on your problems, you become less guarded. You can try out new ideas without the fear of being taken advantage of.

With positive emotions, you are motivated to do more. Things get done more efficiently as you and others work jointly and with increased emotional commitment. You are more open to listening and more open to learning about the other party's interests, making a mutually satisfying outcome within your reach. As a result, your agreement is more likely to be stable over time.

Positive emotions can enhance a relationship. Positive emotions can provide you with the intrinsic enjoyment that comes from a person-to-person interaction. You can enjoy the experience of negotiating and the personal benefits of camaraderie. You can talk comfortably without the fear of getting sidetracked by a personal attack.

That same camaraderie can act as a safety net. It can allow you to disagree with others, knowing that even if things get tense, each of you will be there tomorrow to deal with things.

Positive emotions need not increase your risk of being exploited. Although positive emotions may help you produce a mutually satisfying agreement, there is a danger that you may feel so comfortable that you make unwise concessions or act with overconfidence. Our advice is not to inhibit positive emotions but rather to check with your head and your gut before making decisions. Before committing to an agreement, check that it satisfies your interests. Draw on standards of fairness. Know each person's alternative to a negotiated agreement, and use that information wisely.

Table 1, which follows, contrasts the effect of positive and negative emotions on a negotiation. This table illustrates the effect of emotions on seven key elements of the negotiation process that are described on page 207.

DEALING WITH EMOTIONS:
THREE APPROACHES THAT DON'T WORK

Despite knowing that emotions can harm or help a negotiation, we still have little guidance on how to deal with them. How can we reap their benefits? It is sometimes suggested that negotiators: Stop having emotions; ignore them; or deal directly with them. None of those suggestions helps.

Stop Having Emotions? You Can't.

You cannot stop having emotions any more than you can stop having thoughts. At all times you are feeling some degree of happiness or

TABLE 1

SOME FREQUENT EFFECTS OF EMOTIONS

Elements of Negotiation	Negative Emotions Tend to Foster:	Positive Emotions Tend to Foster:
Relationship	A tense relationship filled with distrust	A cooperative working relationship
Communication	Communication that is limited and confrontational	Open, easy, two-way communication
Interests	Ignoring interests; clinging to an extreme demand; conceding stubbornly if at all	Listening and learning about each other's concerns and wants
Options	Two options: our position or theirs	Creating a lot of possible options that might accommodate some interests of each
	Doubts that options for mutual gain are possible	Optimism that with hard work mutually beneficial options can be created
Legitimacy	A battle of wills over why we are right and they are wrong	Use of criteria that should be persuasive to both why one option is fairer than another
	Fear of being "taken"	A sense of fairness
BATNA (Best Alternative To a Negotiated Agreement)	Walking away from a possible agreement even if our BATNA is worse	Commitment to the best we can get, as long as it is better than our BATNA
Commitments	No agreement, or commitments that are unclear or unworkable	Well-drafted obligations that are clear, operational, and realistic
	Regret for making (or not making) the agreement	Contentment, support, and advocacy for the agreement

sadness, enthusiasm or frustration, isolation or engagement, pain or pleasure. You cannot turn emotions on and off like a light switch.

Consider the experience of "Michele," a researcher who was just offered a job at a big pharmaceutical company. She was initially excited about her compensation—until she discovered that two other recent hires had been offered higher initial salaries. She was upset and confused. From her point of view, her qualifications far outshone theirs.

Michele decided to negotiate for a higher salary. When asked what her negotiation strategy was, she said, "I plan to negotiate 'rationally.' I'm not going to let emotions enter into our conversation. I just want to 'talk numbers.' " She tried to persuade a company executive that if others of equal caliber received a higher salary, she deserved a similar compensation. Good, principled approach. Unfortunately, the negotiation did not go well. Her emotions failed to stop during the negotiation, even though she presumed she had them under control.

As Michele recalls: "The tone of my voice was more abrasive than usual. I didn't want it to be that way. But it was. I felt upset that the company was trying to hire me for less money than the other two new hires. The company's negotiator interpreted my statements as demands. I was surprised when the negotiator said that he refused to be arm twisted into giving a salary raise to *anyone,* let alone a new hire. I wasn't trying to coerce him into a salary raise. But my emotions just didn't switch off the way I had hoped."

In most circumstances, negotiators would be foolish to turn off emotions even if they could. Stopping emotions would make your job harder, not easier. Emotions convey information to you about the relative importance of your concerns. They focus you on those things about which you care personally, such as respect or job security. You also learn what is important to the other side. If the other person communicates an interest with great enthusiasm, you might assume that that interest is important. Rather than spend days trying to understand the other side's interests and priorities, you can save time and energy by learning what you can from their emotions.

Ignore Emotions? It Won't Work.

You ignore emotions at your peril. Emotions are always present and often affect your experience. You may try to ignore them, but they will not ignore you. In a negotiation, you may be only marginally aware of the important ways that emotions influence your body, your thinking, and your behavior.

Emotions affect your body. Emotions can have an immediate impact on your physiology, causing you to perspire, to blush, to laugh, or to feel butterflies in your stomach. After you feel an emotion, you might try to control the expression of that emotion. You might hold back from a smile of excitement or from crying in disappointment. But your body still experiences physiological changes. And suppressing the emotion comes at a cost. A suppressed emotion continues to affect your body. Whether an emotion is negative or positive, internal stress can distract your attention. Trying to suppress that emotion can make it harder to concentrate on substantive issues.

Emotions affect your thinking. When you feel disappointment or anger, your head clogs with negative thoughts. You may criticize yourself or blame others. Negative thinking crowds out space in your brain for learning, thinking, and remembering. In fact, some negotiators become so wrapped up in their own negative emotions and thoughts that they fail to hear their counterpart make an important concession.

When you feel positive emotions, in contrast, your thoughts often center on what is right about you, others, or ideas. With little anxiety that you will be exploited, your thinking becomes more open, creative, and flexible. You become inclined not to reject ideas but to invent workable options.

Emotions affect your behavior. Virtually every emotion you feel motivates you to take action. If you are exuberant, you may feel a physical impulse to hug the other side. If you are angry, you may feel like hitting them.

Usually you can stop yourself before you perform a regrettable action. When you feel a strong emotion, however, careful thinking lags behind, and you may feel powerless to your emotion. In such moments, your ability to censor your thoughts or reflect on possible action is severely limited. You may find yourself saying or doing things that you later regret.

Deal Directly with Emotions? A Complicated Task.

Negotiators are often advised to become aware of emotions—both their own and those of others—and to deal directly with those emotions. Some people are naturally talented at dealing directly with emotions, and most can improve their ability. If a negotiator habitually gets angry, for example, he or she can learn helpful skills to recognize and manage that anger.

Yet even for a trained psychologist or psychiatrist, it is a daunting proposition to deal directly with every emotion as it happens in oneself and others. And trying to deal directly with emotions is particularly challenging when negotiating, where you also need to spend time thinking about each person's differing views on substantive issues and the process for working together. It can feel as though you are trying to ride a bicycle while juggling and talking on a cell phone.

Dealing directly with every emotion as it happens would keep you very busy. As you negotiate, you would have to look for evidence of emotions in yourself and in others. Are you sweating? Are their arms crossed? You would have to infer the many specific emotions taking place in you and in them. (Look through the list of emotion words in Table 2 on page 13 and think how long it takes simply to read through that list, let alone to correctly identify which emotions you and others are feeling.) You would have to make informed guesses about the apparent causes, which may be multiple and unclear. Is the other person upset because of something you said—or because of a fight with a family member this morning?

You would have to decide how to behave, then behave that way, and then notice the emotional impact of that behavior on yourself and on the other person. If the resulting emotions are negative and

TABLE 2

EMOTION WORDS

Positive Emotions	Negative Emotions
Excited	Guilty
Glad	Ashamed
Amused	Humiliated
Enthusiastic	Embarrassed
Cheerful	Regretful
Jovial	
Delighted	Envious
Ecstatic	Jealous
	Disgusted
Proud	Resentful
Gratified	Contemptuous
Happy	
Jubilant	Impatient
Thrilled	Irritated
Overjoyed	Angry
Elated	Furious
	Outraged
Relieved	
Comforted	Intimidated
Content	Worried
Relaxed	Surprised
Patient	Fearful
Tranquil	Panicked
Calm	Horrified
Hopeful	Sad
In awe	Hopeless
Wonder	Miserable
	Devastated

strong, there is a great risk that each person's emotions will quickly escalate.

Emotions are usually contagious. Even if your emotions change from frustration to active interest, the other person is likely to be reacting still to your indignant behavior of a few minutes ago. The impact of a negative emotion lingers long after it has passed. The stronger and more troublesome the emotion, the greater the risk that both of you will lose control.

Thus comes the question to which this book is directed: How should a negotiator cope with the interacting, important, and ever-changing emotions of each side? Given that we cannot realistically be expected to observe, understand, and deal directly with these emotions as they occur, must we simply react as best we can?

AN ALTERNATIVE: FOCUS ON CORE CONCERNS

This book offers negotiators—and that means everyone—a powerful framework for dealing with emotions. Whether or not you acknowledge emotions, they *will* have an impact on your negotiation. As the following chapters suggest, you can avoid reacting to scores of constantly changing emotions and turn your attention to five core concerns that are responsible for many, if not most, emotions in a negotiation. These core concerns lie at the heart of many emotional challenges when you negotiate. Rather than feeling powerless in the face of emotions, you will be able to stimulate positive emotions and overcome negative ones.

CHAPTER 2

Address the Concern, Not the Emotion

Rather than getting caught up in every emotion you and others are feeling, turn your attention to what generates these emotions.

Core concerns are human wants that are important to almost everyone in virtually every negotiation. They are often unspoken but are no less real than our tangible interests. Even experienced negotiators are often unaware of the many ways in which these concerns motivate their decisions.

Core concerns offer you a powerful framework to deal with emotions without getting overwhelmed by them. This chapter provides an overview of how to use them.

FIVE CORE CONCERNS STIMULATE MANY EMOTIONS

Five concerns stimulate, for better or worse, a great many emotions that arise in a negotiation. These core concerns are *appreciation, affiliation, autonomy, status,* and *role.*

When you deal effectively with these concerns, you can stimulate positive emotions both in yourself and in others. Because everyone has these concerns, you can immediately utilize them to stimulate positive emotions. This is true even if you are meeting someone for the first time. You reap the benefits of positive emotions without having to observe, label, and diagnose the scores of ever-changing emotions in yourself and others.

Obviously, powerful feelings can be stimulated by hunger, thirst, lack of sleep, or physical pain. The core concerns, however, focus on your relationship with others. As Table 3 illustrates, each core concern involves how you see yourself in relation to others or how they see themselves in relation to you.

These five core concerns are not completely distinct from one another. They blend, mix, and merge. But each has its own special contribution in stimulating emotions. Together, these concerns more fully describe the emotional content of a negotiation than could any single core concern. The core concerns are analogous to the instruments a quintet uses to play Mozart's Woodwind Quintet. No sharp edges divide the contribution of the flute, oboe, clarinet, bassoon, and French horn. But together, the five instruments more fully capture the tone and rhythm of the music than could any individual instrument.

We want each of the core concerns to be met not excessively nor minimally, but to an *appropriate* extent. Three standards can be used to measure if our concerns are treated appropriately. Do we feel that others are treating our concerns in ways that are:

- *Fair?* Fair treatment is consistent with custom, law, organizational practice, and community expectations. We feel treated as well as others who are in similar or comparable circumstances.

- *Honest?* Honest treatment means that what we are being told is true. We may not be entitled to know everything, but we do not want to be deceived. When the other person honestly

TABLE 3

FIVE CORE CONCERNS

Core Concerns	The Concern Is Ignored When . . .	The Concern Is Met When . . .
Appreciation	Your thoughts, feelings, or actions are devalued.	Your thoughts, feelings, and actions are acknowledged as having merit.
Affiliation	You are treated as an adversary and kept at a distance.	You are treated as a colleague.
Autonomy	Your freedom to make decisions is impinged upon.	Others respect your freedom to decide important matters.
Status	Your relative standing is treated as inferior to that of others.	Your standing where deserved is given full recognition.
Role	Your current role and its activities are not personally fulfilling.	You so define your role and its activities that you find them fulfilling.

addresses our concerns, their intent is not to deceive or trick us. They communicate what they authentically experience or know.

- *Consistent with current circumstances?* It is perhaps unreasonable to expect all of our concerns to be met in every circumstance. Norms change as we deal with everyday matters or a crisis. Appropriate treatment is often consistent with these changing norms.

The difference between having a core concern ignored or met can be as important as having your nose underwater or above it. If, for example, you are unappreciated or unaffiliated, you may feel as if you are drowning, alone, ignored, and unable to breathe. Your emotions respond, and you are prone to adversarial behavior. On the other hand, if you feel appreciated or affiliated, it is as if you are swimming with your head above water. You can breathe easily, look around, and are free to decide what to do and where to go. Your positive emotions are there with you, and, as a result, you are prone to cooperate, to think creatively, and to be trustworthy. (See Table 4 on page 19.)

USE THE CORE CONCERNS AS A LENS AND AS A LEVER

The power of the core concerns comes from the fact that they can be used as both a lens to understand the emotional experience of each party and as a lever to stimulate positive emotions in yourself and in others.

As a Lens to See a Situation More Clearly and to Diagnose It

The core concerns can be used as a lens to help you prepare, conduct, and review the emotional dimension of your negotiation.

Preparing for your negotiation. You can use the core concerns as a checklist of sensitive areas to look for in yourself and in others. In what ways might others be sensitive to what you say or fail to say about their *status*? Will the senior negotiator on the other team feel that her *autonomy* is impinged upon if you revise the current proposal without first consulting her? Do you feel your sense of *affiliation* has been affronted when the rest of the team goes to lunch without inviting you?

Conducting your negotiation. Awareness of the core concerns can help you see what might be motivating a person's behavior. For example, you might realize that the other team's leader feels unappreciated for the many weeks he spent building internal support for the agreement. With that awareness, you can tailor your actions to address his concern.

Awareness of your core concerns can defuse much of the volatility of escalating emotions. If the other party says something that pushes your button, you want to prevent yourself from losing control of your own behavior. Rather than reacting to the perceived attack on you, take a deep breath and ask yourself which of your core concerns

TABLE 4

THE RISK OF *IGNORING* CORE CONCERNS

My Core Concerns Are *Unmet* Whenever:	The Resulting Emotions Can Make Me Feel:		When This Happens, I Am Prone:
I am unappreciated	**Angry!**	**Disgusted**	To react negatively, contrary to my interests
	Enraged	Repulsed	
I am treated as an adversary	Furious	Sickened	
	Indignant	Resentful	
	Irritated	Contemptuous	To "go it alone"
	→Annoyed		
My autonomy is impinged	Hateful	**Guilty and**	To think rigidly
	Spiteful	**Ashamed**	
	Impatient	Remorseful	
My status is put down		Humiliated	To act deceptively and be seen as untrustworthy
	Anxious	Embarrassed	
My role is trivialized and restricted	Regretful		
	Fearful	**Sad**	
	Nervous	Anguished	
	Uneasy	Hopeless	
	Alarmed	Gloomy	
		Devastated	
	Envious and	Apathetic	
	Jealous		

THE POWER OF *MEETING* CORE CONCERNS

My Core Concerns Are *Met* When:	The Resulting Emotions Can Make Me Feel:		When This Happens, I Am Prone:
I am appreciated	**Enthusiastic!**	**Affectionate**	To cooperate
	Cheerful	Fond	
I am treated as a colleague	Playful	Caring	To work together
	Amused	Compassionate	
	Ecstatic		To be creative
		Proud	
My freedom to decide is acknowledged	**Happy**	Accomplished	To be trustworthy
	Content	Courageous	
	Pleased		
My high status is recognized where deserved	Jovial	**Calm**	
	Comforted	Relieved	
	Glad	Relaxed	
My role is fulfilling; it includes activities that convince me that I can make a difference	**Hopeful**		

is being rattled. Is the other negotiator impinging upon your autonomy? Demeaning your status?

Reviewing your negotiation. In reviewing a meeting, you can use the core concerns to help you understand what happened emotionally. If the discussion was cut short because your colleague stormed out of the meeting, you might take a moment to run through the core concerns to try to figure out what may have triggered the other person's anger. You can use this information to address the situation or to prevent its recurrence. If a meeting went surprisingly well, the core concerns can be used to understand what worked. You might develop your own list of best practices.

As a Lever to Help Improve a Situation

Whether or not you know what a person is currently feeling and why, each core concern can be used as a lever to stimulate positive emotions. This is often easier than identifying which of many negative emotions have been stimulated and then determining what to do. You can say or do things that address one of the areas of core concern, moving a negotiator up or down in status, affiliation, autonomy, appreciation, and role. Positive emotions result.

You can also use the core concerns to shift your own emotions in a positive direction. Perhaps you can reduce the pressure of a big decision by reminding yourself that you have the autonomy to accept or reject an agreement with the other team. Or perhaps you can raise your status by sharing with others a relevant area of knowledge.

A big reason to proactively meet the core concerns is to avoid the strong negative emotions that might be generated if those concerns are left unmet. (The joy people experience when they breathe is no match for the distress they experience when they are drowning.)

SUMMARY

The core concerns are human wants that are important to almost everyone in virtually every negotiation. Rather than trying to deal directly with scores of changing emotions affecting you and others, you can turn your attention to five core concerns: appreciation, affiliation, autonomy, status, and role. You can use them as levers to stimulate positive emotions in yourself and in others. If you have time, you also can use them as a lens to understand which concern is unmet and to tailor your actions to address the unmet concern.

The core concerns are simple enough to use immediately, and sophisticated enough to utilize in complex situations. A negotiation that involves multiple parties and high stakes requires an advanced understanding of the five core concerns.

The following chapters consider in depth how to use the power of each core concern both as a lens to understand and as a lever to improve your negotiation.

II

Take the Initiative

CHAPTER 3

Express Appreciation

Find Merit in What Others Think, Feel, or Do—and Show It

Several years ago, Roger was in Tbilisi, working with South Ossetians and the government of Georgia (a former Soviet republic). On his final day, he decided to shop. As he walked down the main street of the city, he saw a woodcarver under an arcade, hard at work carving a small tray. Some of his wares were displayed for sale. Roger stopped to watch. He remembers the interaction as follows:

Of all the wares on display, I was most attracted to the tray on which the woodcarver was working. So I asked, "How much is the tray?"

"It's not finished yet," he replied.

"When will it be finished?" I asked, feeling a small wave of impatience.

"In a couple of days. Then you can buy it."

"I'd like to buy it now—even with the carving still not finished. What is the price if I buy it now unfinished?" (I was, of course, expecting a discounted price.)

"It is not for sale now," the woodcarver responded.

His curt reply irritated me. I had expressed interest in his work, was willing to buy it unfinished, and he gave my offer not a moment's consideration. He gave me barely a moment's consideration. I felt an impulse to insult his work, to insult him, or just to walk away. But instead, I took a deep breath. I realized that I was feeling unappreciated. Disrespected. Put down.

And then it dawned on me. The carver probably felt unappreciated, too. My behavior had perhaps been no better than his. I had expressed no appreciation of him or his views. He might well have felt emotions very much like my own.

"If I were to sell the tray now," said the carver, "the price would have to be higher."

"Why?" I asked, surprised.

He turned to me, smiled, and said, "Selling the tray today would deprive me of the pleasure of finishing it."

Now I smiled. "I'm leaving Tbilisi in the morning. I admire the tray. I admire your work. And now, more than ever, I want the tray to remind me of the carver who takes such pride in his work and such satisfaction in doing it right."

He smiled again, but said nothing.

"In view of my necessary trip," I asked, "would you do a favor to a traveling stranger by letting me buy the tray today, unfinished, at the same price that it would be were you to finish it?"

After a few moments of thinking, he accepted my offer.

APPRECIATION: A CORE CONCERN AND AN ALL-PURPOSE ACTION

As Roger and the woodcarver learned, feeling appreciated is an important concern. Its importance lies in its impact on the one who is appreciated. From corporate CEOs to kindergarten teachers, diplomats to construction workers, everyone wants to be appreciated.

The results of appreciation are simple and direct. If unappreciated, we feel worse. If properly appreciated, we feel better. Our esteem gains in value, just as the stock market appreciates as it gains in value. We become more open to listening and more motivated to cooperate.

Appreciation is not just a noun that labels a concern: It is also an action. To appreciate is a verb. Appreciation takes on an added value as both a core concern and a strategic action since honestly expressing appreciation is often the best way for one person to meet many of the core concerns of another. Thus, *appreciate others* can be taken as a shorthand, all-purpose guide for enlisting helpful emotions in those with whom you negotiate.

If you and the other side appreciate one another, you are more likely to reach a wise agreement than if each side feels unappreciated. In fact, you benefit by helping the other side feel appreciated, whether or not they reciprocate. They will tend to feel more at ease and cooperative. And by appreciating them, you are more likely to foster their appreciation of you.

OBSTACLES TO FEELING APPRECIATED

In most negotiations, three major obstacles inhibit mutual feelings of appreciation. First, each of us may *fail to understand* the other side's point of view. We argue our own perspective but do not learn theirs. As the other person talks, our mind focuses on ideas we want to communicate. With no real listening, no one feels understood.

Second, if we disagree with what the other person is saying, we may *criticize the merit* in whatever they say or do. We assume that part of the job of a negotiator is to put down the other side. All too often, we listen for the weaknesses in what the other person is saying, not for the merit. Yet everyone sees the world through a unique lens, and we feel devalued when our version of the world is unrecognized or dismissed out of hand. If we spent weeks putting a proposal together and the other side merely criticizes it, we are likely to feel discouraged and angry.

Third, each of us may *fail to communicate* any merit we see in the other side's thoughts, feelings, or actions. When either of us hears the other person only criticizing our perspective, we assume our message and its merit were not heard. We end up arguing more forcefully or giving up.

THREE ELEMENTS TO EXPRESS APPRECIATION

Expressing appreciation thus takes more than a simple thank-you. Since we so often fail to appreciate, we need:

- To *understand* each other's point of view;
- To *find merit* in what each of us thinks, feels, or does; and
- To *communicate* our understanding through words and actions.

Understand Their Point of View

To appreciate another person, your first task is to understand how things look and feel from their point of view. Your main tools are your ability to listen and to ask good questions.

Many people assume *you* cannot really understand how *they* see things unless you have heard it directly from *them*. While that is often true, you can anticipate quite a bit by imagining how you might feel in their shoes. But even if you do understand their point of view, they still may want to be heard. Be prepared to listen.

During a negotiation, there are many active listening techniques you can use to improve your understanding of another. Two are worth noting here:

Listen for the "music" as well as the words. The process of coming to understand is not limited to hearing specific words that someone utters. It is important for a listener to gather the ambience that surrounds them, to listen for the mood, character, atmosphere, and emotional tone that put the words into a context.

Like listening to a song, it is not enough to get the words right. You want to listen for what is accompanying the words—the underlying melody. Just as the crash of a drum can turn a sentimental love song into an angst-ridden war cry, the emotional tone may confirm a negotiator's words or refute them as when a person shouts, "I am *not* angry!"

Listen for "meta-messages." As you listen, you will notice that sometimes one message is buried inside another. Such inexplicit meta-messages occur all the time. At a dinner party, for example, a host may look at his watch and say, "I have been so enjoying myself that I did not realize how late it has become." Most guests quickly catch the meta-message that the party is now over.

Meta-messages often suggest whether a person feels supportive, ambivalent, or resistant to ideas being discussed. An easy way to detect meta-messages is to listen for which word is emphasized. Though the following four sentences are comprised of the same words, each sentence suggests a different meaning. Possible translations are in brackets.

I like this proposal. [But others are resistant.]

I *like* this proposal. [I enthusiastically support this idea.]

I like *this* proposal. [I like this proposal better than others.]

I like this *proposal*. [As a proposal; I am not making a commitment.]

Do not ignore ambivalence or resistance. A person's body language may express something quite different from what words communicate. By being aware of a mixed or meta-message, you can better appreciate another's point of view.

Find Merit in What the Other Person Thinks, Feels, or Does

The second element of appreciation is to find merit. This means that we look for value in what the other person thinks, feels, or does. Just think about what happens around the house. Whether we are cleaning up the kitchen, making the beds, cutting the grass, or remembering a special day, if such efforts go unnoticed or are never outwardly valued, we feel let down. Table 5 illustrates how we might find merit in—and express appreciation for—what another person thinks, feels, or has done.

When views conflict, find merit in their reasoning. Even if you disagree with the other person's stance on an issue, you can acknowledge their reasons for seeing the world as they do. They might be motivated by strong feelings, a passionate belief, or a persuasive argument.

Consider the situation Roger experienced while representing the federal government in front of the U.S. Supreme Court. He stood to make his arguments against the petitioner. Stepping forward he said, "The petitioner has a strong case. In fact, I think it is stronger than the one made by counsel here this morning. If I had been arguing for the petitioner, I would have added the following point. . . ."

"Mr. Fisher!" Justice Frankfurter interrupted. "You are here *for the government!*"

"Yes, Your Honor," Roger said. "And I want the Court to understand that we have an answer not only to the arguments that petitioner has made but also to another good argument that I think petitioner could make. Either way, their case is not trivial or farfetched. We believe this Court was right to grant review and to consider this case on its merits as we in the government have. Despite the strength of their case, we have concluded that the law is against them for reasons that I will now present . . ."

Roger believed that by honestly expressing his appreciation for the merits of his opponent's case, he was a more effective advocate for the government than if he had squared off, contending that the petitioner's arguments were absurd and should be dismissed out of hand. Having demonstrated a thorough understanding of the other side's case—and directly answering it—his argument was likely to be more effective than if he simply avoided their contention and made an argument of his own. (The government won the case.)

This way of expressing appreciation also convinced the petitioner's lawyers that they had been heard and that their arguments

TABLE 5
WHERE TO FIND MERIT

Find Merit in What Another Person:	Illustrative Statement
Thinks	
Logic and reasoning	"I find your arguments persuasive."
Points of view	"Even though I disagree with your conclusion, I see value in your point of view."
Feels	
Emotions	"I admire the pride you put into your work."
Core concerns	"I think it makes sense that you don't want to be excluded from tomorrow's meeting."
Does	
Actions	"I value what you do around here."
Effort	"I appreciate your putting together this first draft."

had merit. At the end of the day, counsel for petitioner came across the courtroom to Roger, shook his hand, and thanked him for treating their arguments so seriously.

Finding merit in another's reasoning requires that you actually *do* see merit in it. Sincerity is crucial. It is your honest valuing of another's perspective that makes them feel appreciated. You want to express that you understand the basis for why they feel, think, or act the way they do. While you may struggle to find value in what they say or do, look hard and imagine what their emotional experience is like, considering what concerns may be motivating their emotions.

When you strongly disagree with others, try acting like a mediator. The hardest time to find merit in another's point of view is when you are arguing about an issue that may be personally important. Listening for merit in another's point of view can transform the way you listen.

To do this, try acting like an impartial mediator. A mediator works to understand each disputant's perspective and to look for the value in it. In this role, you refrain from judging whose side is right or wrong. Instead, you try to see the merit in *each* side's perspective.

To take on the perspective of a mediator, start by discovering why the other person's view on an issue may be personally important and persuasive to them. What beliefs and reasoning underlie their view? You may not agree with their stance on the issue, but you can still find merit in the reasoning and beliefs that brought them to that conclusion. Once you find merit, you will be able to say:

I understand [*your point of view*], and I appreciate [*your reasoning or beliefs*].

Consider the example of a pro-choice leader searching for merit in a pro-life leader's point of view. She probably won't find value in the leader's stance that abortion should be illegal. But she might be able to see merit in some of the reasons and beliefs underlying that stance. She might say:

I understand that you believe that life begins at conception. [*She demonstrates understanding.*]
And with this as a core belief, I can see the value in your wanting to protect what you see as an innocent child. [*She shows that she sees merit in the other person's reasoning.*]

Appreciation is not something to be bargained over. In fact, it loses much of its value if my expressing appreciation of your point of view is made conditional on your expressing appreciation of mine. If the pro-life leader were to go through the same process—finding and expressing some merit in the pro-choice leader's reasoning—then each side would feel appreciated. And neither person changes her basic beliefs about abortion. In fact, each leader may become clearer and firmer in her own views. Thus, by seeing merit in the other side's reasoning, the leaders can simultaneously disagree and work together. They might, for example, decide to initiate a joint project aimed at reducing unwanted pregnancies.

There may be persuasive reasons for your being unwilling to see some merit in the views of another. We have found two. The first is that to do so appears to be contrary to your religious beliefs. The second is that to express such merit could easily be misunderstood by your friends, family, or constituents. They might think that your seeing merit demonstrates that you agree with views with which you, in fact, disagree.

Communicate Your Understanding

The third element of expressing appreciation is to demonstrate your understanding of the merit you have found. Once you understand their perspective and find merit, let them know. Your remarks should be apt; fitting; to the point; appropriate to the circumstances; and, above all, honest. There is no need for flowery language. What is important is that the person's thoughts, feelings, or actions are recognized and acknowledged. Plain and simple.

It sounds like you feel worried that if you sell your shares of stock, your relationships with other members of the board would be damaged. *[You demonstrate your understanding.]*

I can appreciate your concern, especially given that you want to keep working in this industry. *[You show that you see merit in the other person's reasoning.]*

To ensure that the other person does not become defensive, express your message in an affirming tone. This is easier if you already have found merit in their perspective. Rather than saying in a sarcastic voice, "Yes, I understand the reason why *you* think you deserve a pay raise," you can affirm their perspective:

I think you have good reason to feel you deserve a pay raise. You have invested significant time in this company. You've worked hard. You have successfully managed projects involving two of our biggest clients.

Both the sarcastic statement and the affirmative one indicate that you understand what the other person is saying. Yet only the second statement demonstrates that you see merit in the other person's point of view. And validating their perspective does not mean that you are giving in.

Reflect back what you hear. It is rarely enough simply to understand another or even to say, "Yes. I understand." Others are likely to feel unheard unless you demonstrate to them that you *do* in fact understand what it is that they believe is important. This is a lesson learned by two leaders with whom Dan worked. As he recalls:

I was in Lake Ohrid, Macedonia, facilitating a week-long negotiation workshop for social and political leaders. Participants included ethnic Albanians and Macedonians. At the time of the workshop, violence had erupted between these groups. The war in Kosovo had triggered an influx of thousands of Albanians into Macedonia. Some Macedonians feared a loss of political and cultural influence.

During a coffee break, I sat at a table with two participants, "Ivan," a Macedonian, and "Bamir," an ethnic Albanian. They immediately started to argue.

"Do you realize that thousands and thousands of Albanian refugees have come here from Kosovo?" said Ivan. "How are we supposed to take care of that many people?"

"What's the choice?" Bamir responded. "You don't know what it feels like to be in a hopeless situation like ours."

"Look," said Ivan, "if we don't help those refugees, the world will think we're ruthless. But our country's too small. What are we supposed to do?"

"You don't understand the situation," says Bamir. "You

don't know what it feels like to be rejected by your own country!"

Back and forth the two men argued. Their voices got louder. They talked over one another. I had initially listened to learn their perspectives, but now things were getting out of hand.

I cut in and said, "Hold on a minute. This is getting nowhere."

They stopped for a moment and looked at me. I said, "You both seem frustrated. Let's try to figure things out."

"He just doesn't get my situation!" interrupted Bamir.

"He's the one who doesn't understand!" snapped Ivan.

I paused for a moment. We all calmed down. "Ivan," I said, "What did you learn from listening to Bamir?"

He began, "Bamir thinks that Macedonians reject ethnic Albanians. And we don't."

"That's not what I said *at all*!"

I asked Bamir, "What did you hear Ivan saying?"

"It's obvious that he only wants to take care of *his* people."

Ivan jumped in and said, "That's not what *I* said at all!"

The two men stared blankly at one another. They had listened, but they had not heard one another. Neither knew what the other one was saying nor responded to it. They were having two separate conversations, each responding to his own assumptions and emotions.

There was silence. Then Ivan laughed. He realized what had happened, and the realization startled him. He said, "Nobody gets anywhere if we close our ears."

And he is right. All too often, people fail to listen because they want their turn to speak and express themselves. Listening is not passive, but active. It takes concentration. During the rest of the workshop, I watched as Bamir and Ivan tried to listen— to really listen—to one another. On more than one occasion, their emotions still overrode their ability to listen. But they were now *trying* to find merit in each other's perspective—and to let one another know.

If you find that you have stopped listening to the other person, ask yourself, "Am I done or are they done?" In other words, have you prematurely stopped listening to the other person—perhaps because you are tired of listening to them or are uncomfortable with the emotions they are expressing?

Reflective listening motivates you to listen carefully. You paraphrase either the factual information or the feelings the other person is expressing. Dan demonstrated reflective listening when he said to the men, "You both seem frustrated." This allowed Ivan and Bamir to feel heard.

Suggest how upset you might be if it happened to you. We are often unable to assess accurately the emotions that are affecting another person. If we try, we may misread the other person's emotions and offend him or her.

This happened to a tenant who wanted to negotiate the rent for her apartment. The landlord was a lawyer who lived in the apartment below her. The tenant decided to begin the negotiation by trying to build rapport. She said, "I heard you just switched to a new law firm. That must be tough."

The landlord's face turned pale, and he snapped, "No. That's not the case. Now tell me why you want to meet with me." As he said these words, a different set of ideas cluttered his head. He worried, "Is she implying that I'm not strong enough to handle a job change? How weak does she think I am?" Despite the tenant's good intentions, the landlord felt criticized and offended.

A nonintrusive approach would be to assume only how we would feel if the situation happened to us. This is best done after asking the other how they are feeling. The tenant could say, "I heard about your job switch. What's it been like? If I had to switch jobs, I know I'd find it tough." Such a vicarious suggestion tends to open the way for better communication. In this less presumptuous approach, she remains open to learning, and the landlord no longer feels that an emotional experience is being imposed upon him.

TO APPRECIATE DOES NOT MEAN TO GIVE IN

Many people fear that appreciating someone's point of view is equivalent to agreeing with them. Wrong. Whether or not you agree with someone, you can find merit in their reasoning and let them know. You give up none of your authority to decide; you can still say yes or no to proposals and increase the likelihood that the two of you will be able to work effectively together.

It is possible for you to *understand* a person's ideas or opinions that you think are foolish or patently wrong. It is also possible to understand, for example, arguments that you believe are weighty, important, and deserving of attention even if you happen to disagree with them or feel that they are outweighed by other factors. Communicating that you understand is quite different from saying, "I agree with you" or "I will do what you suggest."

For example, a lawyer can interview a client and demonstrate understanding of the client's emotional difficulties. This does not mean, however, that the lawyer agrees with every action or opinion of the client. But he or she can appreciate the underlying beliefs and reasoning. To prevent misunderstanding, the lawyer might preface the conversation by saying, "I want to understand, to really understand, more about your experience so that I can best represent you. I may not agree with everything you say or have done, but I want you to be confident that I do see merit in your point of view."

In business, too, it can be helpful to appreciate another person while, at the same time, not giving in to them. Consider the case of "Mark," a talented manager at an automobile manufacturing company, who was struck with Parkinson's disease. As the disease progressed, he lost his ability to speak clearly and to keep his balance. He had fallen several times at work, but fortunately had not hurt himself.

Mark was friendly with the leadership of the organization, especially "Sam," the regional president, whose family had joined Mark's family for the past four years' summer vacations. Mark suspected that the leadership wanted him to take early retirement due to his impaired ability to communicate with employees. Mark wanted to semiretire. He loved his job, but wanted to spend winters with his wife at a home near the beach. He certainly did not want senior management to dictate unilaterally the terms of his departure. Rather than making demands of the senior management and risk turning the situation into an adversarial battle, Mark used the power of appreciation. He set up a private meeting with the CEO and said:

> Sam, thanks for taking the time to meet. I've been thinking about how to manage my work life now that this disease is starting to make communication more of a challenge. We've been good friends for a long time, and I'm sure this is hard for you to see the disease affect me as it has. I know you want to look out for my best interest and to make sure that I don't put too much stress on myself. I also assume that, as regional president, you need to look out for the company's best interests. You want people to satisfy their daily responsibilities efficiently. So I'd imagine that this situation is hard for you. I wanted to sit down with you and, without committing to anything, just think through some options we have.

Through these statements, Mark demonstrates an understanding of Sam's point of view without conceding anything. Rather, he recognizes that Sam cares about him and that Sam also has professional responsibilities to uphold. These statements promote a positive tone to their conversation and increase the likelihood that an outcome will satisfy the interests of Mark, Sam, and the company.

PREPARE TO APPRECIATE OTHERS

Now that you know *how* to appreciate others, you can get ready to do it. Although you cannot read a negotiator's mind, you can do a lot to get a better sense of how things look and feel from their perspective.

Decide Who You Want to Appreciate

Your first step is to decide *who* you want to appreciate. Regardless of a person's age, wealth, or authority, every person values appreciation. It is a core concern that is shared by people from the top to the bottom. We often assume that the person above us in rank or command does not need appreciation. Appreciation is supposed to be one way—from the top down, right? No. Subordinates need appreciation, and so do superiors. You can appreciate your boss, your subordinates, your peers, and even those with whom you are negotiating. In fact, in situations where you feel disempowered, your appreciation of others can level the playing field. When another person feels truly heard, you have valued not only the person's message but also the person as an individual.

Roger recalls an experience when he learned about the power of appreciating those higher and lower in the chain of command. In 1949, he was working in Paris for the Marshall Plan, the postwar economic recovery program for Europe. "Barry," the finance officer in Paris and Roger's good friend, had been working for weeks on a plan to deal with a potential financial crisis in Austria.

One Monday morning, the Paris *Herald Tribune* reported that there was indeed a financial crisis. All banks in Austria were closed, and Ambassador Averell Harriman, head of the Marshall Plan for Europe, had flown to Vienna to deal with the crisis. Because Harriman left quickly for Austria, he had no chance to talk first with Barry about the situation.

By the end of the week, Harriman resolved the crisis (brilliantly, Barry reported).

Yet Barry felt unappreciated and unneeded. Harriman apparently had resolved the crisis without getting Barry's input. Barry had spent weeks preparing ideas, but they were of no use. He told Roger he was thinking of quitting his job.

The following week, Roger was working with Harriman on another matter when Harriman asked him to sit down and tell him about morale among the younger staff.

Roger said, "Sometimes people don't feel valued. Barry told me how well you had done in Austria without him. He's now thinking of looking for another job."

"Barry?" the Ambassador said. "That guy's a genius. When the call from Vienna came in on Saturday afternoon, I phoned Barry, but he wasn't home. With the help of security, we searched his office, and in his safe we found a forty-page draft memorandum about what to do if there was a financial crisis in Austria. I made a photocopy of the memo, which I took with me. It was my 'bible' all week. I simply followed his advice, and it worked."

"Have you told Barry?"

"No. He was just doing his job. I'm not here to thank people for doing what they are paid to do. You can tell him if you like."

Roger called Harriman's secretary into the inner office and, in front of Harriman, said, "Would you please find ten or fifteen minutes on the Ambassador's schedule so the finance officer can hear from the Ambassador what he just told me."

"No," said Ambassador Harriman.

"Yes!" Roger said to his top boss, a man who was twice his age. "It is important."

"No one ever tells *me* that I am doing a great job," said Harriman.

Roger was dumbfounded. "I never thought of it as appropriate for *me* to be telling *you* what a terrific job you're doing. Of course, you do come to the office late in the mornings. But by the time you come, you have already read all the overnight cables from Washington and from the missions and have figured out what to do. And you work late. Here we are still working at 8:30 P.M. 'in the afternoon' as you call it."

Ambassador Harriman may have learned as a boy to make his bed and to do other chores without expecting any thanks. But that did not mean that he did not *want* the appreciation. Later, as an adult, he may not have given appreciation to others because he himself had little hope of receiving it.

Try the Role Reversal Exercise

Prepare to appreciate another person's point of view by trying the Role Reversal Exercise. Work with a colleague who can help you enter the role of the person whom you would like to appreciate. You "become" that person. Your colleague can ask you questions to help you understand what the person on the other side of the table might be experiencing.

"What do you [*in the role of the other party*] most care about?"

"About what concerns are you particularly sensitive?"

"Of course money is important, but please explain: What other things do you care about? Respect? Acceptance? Being heard?"

In response to each question, you answer in the first person as though you really were the absent party. For example, "I feel upset when others ignore my opinions." By using role reversal early on, your colleague can help you step into the shoes of someone whom you would like to appreciate.

Dan remembers how role reversal helped a mother cope with a difficult marital conflict. When her grown son called saying that he was moving back to town, "Ana" did not think twice before saying, "Why don't you stay with us until you find a place?" At the time, she had no idea that her offer would bring up issues that would jeopardize her fifteen-year, second marriage. Barely able to contain her excitement, Ana told her husband, "Joe," the good news. To her surprise, he was angry at her for inviting her son to move back in.

"Why can't you be excited about this?" she asked her husband.

"I don't want him here indefinitely," he said. "They've left the nest. Now it's time for us to be together."

"He won't be living in our house forever," Ana said.

"Knowing him, he'll make himself at home," Joe said. "He's in his late twenties now. He's an adult . . ."

"But don't you want our family around?" Ana asked. "Or is it that this is *my* child and not yours?"

"I don't care whose kid it is! They're just too old to be moving back here."

Ana suddenly had an awful feeling that this was not the man she married, the good father with whom she had raised her children and his. She was furious and confused; she felt as though she had to choose between her husband and her son. She got up and left the room.

Tension escalated. Living together was almost intolerable. They began yelling at each other, something they had never done before. Ana turned to Dan for advice. After explaining the situation to him, they talked about a process for moving forward:

I said, "You and Joe sound like two ships passing in the night. Neither of you seems to really understand the other person's point of view. And it's leaving each of you feeling unappreciated."

She nodded and asked, "So what can I do about it?"

I said, "You both have an interest in wanting this relationship to work out. You can start by trying to appreciate Joe's perspective. Let's try an exercise to help you do that." I asked her to answer three questions from Joe's point of view. Here are the questions, as well as what she discovered.

1. **"In what ways might Joe feel that you do not understand him?"** Ana recognized that she acted as though the son was hers alone. She accused Joe of not caring for the son because he was not related by blood ("Is it that this is *my* child and not yours?"). She had defended her own point of view and made little effort to understand his.

2. **"In what ways might Joe's point of view have merit?"**
   Ana imagined what the situation might feel like from Joe's perspective. She realized that having a child under their roof may have awakened Joe's memories of round-the-clock responsibility for teaching the children how to do everything from riding a bicycle to reading a book. At this time in Joe's life, he probably wanted to reduce "extra" responsibilities and enjoy time alone with his wife.

3. **"Have you communicated your understanding to Joe?"**
   Ana realized her failure to communicate what merit she saw in Joe's perspective. She was afraid that by communicating merit, she would be conceding to his views. She never acknowledged any understanding of his fears and wishes.

Ana then tried to appreciate her own point of view. She came to *understand* that the pressures of her role as wife and mother pulled her in two different directions: to support her son and to care for her marriage. She found *merit* in her point of view. She was trying to satisfy emotionally both her son and her husband. She wanted Joe to *communicate his understanding* of her concerns and the merit in them.

Preparation gave Ana increased understanding of the conflict. Rather than criticizing her husband, she was now ready to listen and to learn. To change the tone of their negotiation, she prepared one simple question: "Help me understand. Where are you coming from on this?"

Once she asked the question, Ana listened to the answer without judgment. She learned that her husband was protective of their marital relationship. He had looked forward to the time when their house would be all theirs and the two of them could spend "endless" hours together. She also learned that having an adult child around would make him jealous for her time.

Because she listened to her husband and communicated her understanding until he felt heard, the tone of their interaction shifted.

Joe felt that his wife loved him deeply and that she appreciated the need to set aside time for just the two of them. He learned that she felt a parental obligation to help her son, who recently had broken up with his girlfriend. And he discovered how much she missed playing the role of mother and watching him play the role of father to their children.

There were no easy answers to their problems, but they were now negotiating their differences side by side. Their discussion became a source of mutual learning. After some time, they were able to comfortably negotiate an arrangement where the son would live with them for one month, which was enough time for him to find an apartment.

Prepare a List of "Good Questions" to Learn Another Person's Perspective

As a negotiator, you would be well-advised to develop your own personal list of generic questions to learn more about another's perspective. These might be questions that were prepared for a different negotiation—whether used or not—or good questions that were asked of you by another negotiator. Ana's question to Joe, "Help me understand. Where are you coming from on this?" is a good example of a generic question that can be used in almost any negotiation. Other such questions include:

"Help me understand how you see things."
"Of all the things we've talked about today, what do you see as most important?"
"What are some of the other things that you care a lot about in this negotiation?"

Too often, negotiators grill one another with questions that try to prove the other side wrong. Each negotiator treats the other negotiator as though he or she were on the witness stand. Such questions call for a short yes or no answer:

"Did you even *think* about the impact of your behavior on my
  client?"
"Are you planning to go behind my back *again*?"

To pursue a wiser goal of coming to understand the other person's perspective, you will want to use *open questions*. Not arguments, but honest inquiries. Such questions invite others to talk
about what they consider important. Open questions typically begin
with the words *how* or *what*. For example:

"You tell me that the house my client is thinking of buying is
   worth at least the $500,000 asking price. What compara-
   ble sales or other information do you have that led you to
   reach that opinion on value?"
"What do you see as some of the advantages of this option?
   What are some of the risks?"
"How do you feel things are going?"
"What are some of your concerns about this proposal?"

HELP OTHERS APPRECIATE YOU

What should you do if a person fails to appreciate you? A negotiation
may feel lopsided and unequal if you are trying to find merit in their
point of view, but they fail to value yours. In resentment, you might
think that you should bargain over appreciation: "I won't express appreciation of him unless he appreciates me." But, as mentioned earlier, this won't work well because appreciation should be sincere.
You are likely to view with suspicion any appreciation given only by
request.

Don't get discouraged. There are plenty of things you can do to
help others *understand* what you are saying, *find merit* in it, and
communicate their understanding. Here are some:

Help Others Understand Your Point of View

If you think that others do not understanding your message, take action.

Propose a specific amount of time for them to listen to you. You can let someone with whom you are working know that you have a particular point on which you would like to be heard. Roger remembers a time when three minutes made all the difference.

John Laylin was the partner at the law firm of Covington & Burling for whom I worked for a number of years as an associate. He and I had each prepared a draft of a letter that our client in Pakistan might send to an Indian official. We each read and commented on the other's draft. Mr. Laylin decided that we would work on his draft. I believed that he had failed to understand why I thought that his was a poor draft. I told him that I thought we should work on mine. He said no—we would work on his. Did I have any changes to suggest?

I asked him to give me three minutes to explain what I thought was wrong with his draft. He resisted. Then he took out his pocket watch, put it on the desk in front of him, and said, "All right. You have three minutes." I had been speaking for only two when he interrupted me, asked why I had not been equally clear earlier, and dropped his draft into the waste basket. We went to work on improving the draft I had prepared.

I was heard. I made my point, and it was persuasive.

Tailor your message to be heard. On the front of many ambulances in the United States, the word *ambulance* is written backward. This allows drivers who look in their rearview mirror to see the word correctly. The person who conceived of this idea wisely considered, "How can we tailor our message so that other drivers get it right?"

In a negotiation, you want to shape your message so that others get it right. You may tell your junior associates that you will give them a 5 percent commission on every item they sell. You think that is generous. What many of them may hear is that you are keeping 95 percent of everything. They interpret the act as greedy. Your message and its intent have not been clearly communicated.

When your emotions or theirs become strong, it can be difficult to communicate your message so that others will hear it. When you are angry, for example, you may have a desire to blame the other side for your negative feelings. "I'm angry because you didn't consult me before signing the agreement." Don't blame. It makes others defensive. Their ability to listen declines as they develop counterarguments in their mind about why *they* are right and *you* are wrong. The ability to work together is reduced.

Rather, you can communicate your anger as part of a forward-looking message. Let the other person know that you are expressing your anger in order to change future interactions. "I'm angry—and I'm letting you know—because I want to be consulted in the future before you sign an agreement that affects both of us." Your chance of being appreciated in the long run is likely to be greater if you want to be heard not just to score points, but because you have a message designed to affect the future.

Help Others Find Merit in What You Think, Feel, or Do

There are actions you can take to help others find merit in your point of view and your emotional experience.

Ask the other person to find merit in your point of view. Rather than argue the merit in your point of view, ask the other person questions. Get him or her to reflect on the merit in your point of view. You might say, "I'm not sure that I have been as clear as I can be about my own perspective. Why do you think I find my own stance on these issues to be important and persuasive?"

Draw on a metaphor that resonates with them. You may feel angry if another person devalues your emotional experience. They might pretend not to notice that you are upset, or they might try to outdo your emotions with their own gripes. How can you encourage them to find value in your emotional experience?

A powerful approach to defuse tensions is to introduce a metaphor into a conversation. A metaphor allows you and others to talk about your shared emotional experience without doing so directly and explicitly. Rather than saying, "I feel anxious about our situation, frustrated by you, annoyed with my colleagues, and pretty hopeless right now," you can talk about your experience using a metaphor. "It feels as though we are dancing to different music."

Either alone or with others, you can create a metaphor that depicts your shared emotional experience. Here is a sampling of such metaphors:

> "We seem to be walking a tightrope here. Let's make sure we have a safety net."
> "I feel as if we're caught in a tide that is pulling us into dangerous waters. Let's change course."
> "I feel like we're walking into a windstorm. How can we keep from moving in that direction?"
> "I feel like we're digging ourselves deeper and deeper into a hole. How can we get out of this?"
> "I feel we're trying to swim upstream. How can we make this easier for both of us?"
> "A chill seems to have come over this room. Can you help me warm things up a bit?"

Metaphors provide a common language for you and others to work through your differences. Through the use of metaphor, you can both acknowledge emotional obstacles and turn those obstacles into problems you can deal with. If you and others are "dancing to different music," you might ask, "How can we synchronize our moves better? Should we take a short break, then come back and see if we're more in step with one another?" If you and others have "hit a roadblock," you might ask, "How can we get around this roadblock? Should we back up our conversation and review your interests and ours?"

Metaphors are commonly used by politicians, news reporters, and negotiators to provide people with a visual, visceral sense of purpose. In the conflict between Israelis and Palestinians, for example, the concept of a road map to peace was initiated jointly by the United States, the European Union, the United Nations, and Russia. The concept of a road map resonated with many people around the world who saw the disputants as being "lost" in conflict. The road map provided a set of suggested activities each side could take. Rather than just saying, "We're announcing a new plan for everyone to consider," the tangible nature of a road map gave the public and politicians a concrete item to grasp and to discuss.

Help Others Hear Your Message

There are a couple of ways to motivate others to listen to you.

Have only a few big points. In crafting a message to be heard, simplify it. You want to be able to answer a few important questions:

Who is the person for whom the message is intended?
What are they supposed to do? Will they understand that?
What are the pros and cons of that choice as *they* will see them?
Are they likely to welcome the message or ignore it?

Answer these questions succinctly and you will have built a strong, clear case for yourself.

Ask them what they hear you saying. You will not know if others are understanding your message unless they let you know. A simple way to find out what they hear you saying is to ask them. You might say, "I'm not sure I'm communicating my message clearly. What do you hear me saying?" If they reflect back your message inaccurately, you can clarify. And whether or not they are accurate, this question motivates them to listen more carefully in the future.

THE IMPORTANCE OF SELF-APPRECIATION

There is a danger in relying on others to appreciate you. You do not have control over their actions. If they fail to give you appreciation, you may feel frustrated. They may even use appreciation as a manipulative tool, flattering you to influence your compliance with a request. Or they may refuse to understand your point of view. Any such actions will push your button if you rely on others for appreciation.

You *do,* however, have control over your ability to appreciate others—*and* over your ability to appreciate yourself. You can use your own internal resources to appreciate yourself, to boost your self-confidence, and to clarify your understanding of your point of view and theirs.

You will want to explore the objective merits of your views and actions, independent of a bias in your favor. Where your views deserve praise, do not hesitate to let yourself know. If you have a difficult time finding areas of value in your own actions or reasoning, imagine how an important mentor in your life would appreciate you. Perhaps you have a parent, teacher, or colleague who has supported you and boosted your esteem in difficult times. What might that person say to you as you are negotiating? Tell yourself that. How might they communicate their valuing of your efforts and views? Listen to that voice.

Where, on reflection, you should qualify your self-praise, do so. Be honest with yourself. It costs you nothing. In fact, you can take pride in your willingness to make a candid appraisal of yourself. This is true whether the result is enthusiastic endorsement of your thinking or honest recognition that, at this point, your ideas are best considered tentative and deserving of rigorous rethinking. The more honestly you appreciate the ideas of another negotiator—both their possible flaws and their merits—and with equal rigor examine your own ideas for their merits and possible weaknesses, the better equipped you and others will be to reach a workable agreement.

It may well be that you have little or no interest in building a long-term relationship with the other negotiator. Of course, one consequence of expressing appreciation of another is that you might change your mind about that. In any event, a better understanding of both the other negotiator and yourself will make it easier for each of you to work together in a way that will result in an agreement.

SUMMARY

Appreciation is a core concern. Everyone has a desire to feel understood, valued, and heard. If people feel honestly appreciated, they are more likely to work together and less likely to act hostile.

You can appreciate by:

- *understanding* a person's point of view;
- *finding merit* in what the person thinks, feels, or does;
- *communicating your understanding* through words or actions.

You may not agree with the other person's point of view. That is fine. But, you can understand it and acknowledge whatever merit you can find.

The chapter on appreciation comes first in this book because we all become emotionally rewarded when we are appreciated just for who we are and what we do. It is also important for us that others appreciate the emotional concern we have for affiliation, autonomy, status, and role. In the following chapters, we share our advice on dealing with these remaining four core concerns.

CHAPTER 4

Build Affiliation

Turn an Adversary into a Colleague

When training a group of negotiators, we often start with the Arm Exercise. In a group with whom we were working one day, there were thirty participants, all with a background in international trade negotiations. We paired them up, one on one, and instructed them to sit down across from their partner, more or less facing each other, with their right elbows on the table. We told them to grab their partner's right hand with their own right hand and not to let go. Each person would get one point every time the back of the other's right hand touched the table. The goal of each was to get as many points for himself or herself as possible during the exercise. Participants were told that they were to be totally indifferent to how many points their partner got . . . and to keep their eyes closed.

"Get ready . . . GO!"

For two minutes, the pairs struggled as each member tried by physical strength to force the back of the other's right hand down to the table. With a lot of effort and against the physical opposition of each partner, almost no one got more than a point or two.

There was a single exception. One participant remembered, almost immediately, that his goal was to get as many points as he could for himself—and that he was wholly *indifferent to how many points his partner got.* Instead of pushing on his partner's hand, he pulled it down to the table, gave his surprised partner a quick and easy point, took a quick point for himself, and then gave his partner another point. Without talking to each other, the two partners, with their elbows on the table, then swung their clasped hands harmoniously back and forth as rapidly as they could, collecting a large number of points for each of them.

We stopped the exercise and had participants report to the group how many points each had obtained. No participant in the group had received more than three points, except for the pair who had cooperated, each of whom had obtained more than twenty.

In our post-exercise review it became apparent that, despite our using the word *partner* and despite our clear instruction that they were to be indifferent to how many points their partner obtained, virtually all participants made the assumption that they and the one with whom they were doing the exercise were adversaries. That adversarial assumption dominated their thinking and prevented them from getting as many points as they could have.

The assumption that the one with whom you are negotiating is an adversary dominates a great many negotiations. And that assumption typically prevents everyone from doing as well as they might.

THE POWER OF AFFILIATION

When negotiating, we are dealing with actual or possible differences with someone else. We want to deal with those differences in a way that leaves us feeling satisfied and that wastes as little time and as few resources as possible. This process is best accomplished when we work together. Using our combined brainpower and understanding, we are well situated to create a mutually satisfying outcome.

A big part of working together involves affiliation. The word *affiliation* comes from the Latin verb, *affiliate,* meaning "to adopt or receive into a family." As a core concern, affiliation describes our sense of connectedness with another person or group. It is the emotional space between us and them. If we feel affiliated with a person or group, we experience little emotional distance. We feel "close."

When we feel affiliated with one another, working together is easier. We view another not as a stranger, but rather as part of the "family." As a result, each of us tends to care for the other, protect the other's interests, and look out for their good. There is less resistance to fresh ideas and more openness to the prospect of changing our mind. Loyalty to one another often keeps us honest, obligates us to search for an agreement of mutual benefit, and makes it likely that we will honor an agreement.

Affiliation involves an *honest* connection. It only happens when someone has a true concern for our well-being, not only for our money. Con artists and telemarketers may try to build affiliation to get our money. But the moment we sense that they do not care about us, we are likely to hang up the phone.

TOO OFTEN, WE OVERLOOK OPPORTUNITIES TO BUILD AFFILIATION

Despite the power of affiliation, we often neglect to build it. Sometimes, we fail to recognize *structural connections* we share with others—the roles that place us in a common group. We and our negotiating counterpart may both be coin collectors, which might bond us together; but if we never discover our common role, we obtain no emotional benefit. We may also disregard our own power to establish *new* roles that link us together as colleagues, fellow negotiators, or joint problem solvers.

Whatever the structure of a relationship, we often fail to strengthen our *personal connections*—the emotional ties that bring us closer to a specific person. Brothers and sisters who live in different communities may drift apart and rarely communicate. Yet, strangers who happen to sit next to one another on a long airline flight may, within hours, be exchanging personal stories that they have not shared with good friends. In a negotiation, the power of a personal connection can bridge the gap between "our side" and theirs.

Enhancing your affiliations is within your reach. In this chapter, we show you how. We begin by suggesting ways to improve your structural connection with others. Next, we offer ideas on how to build your personal connections. We close by advising you on how to protect yourself from having others use affiliation to exploit you.

IMPROVING YOUR STRUCTURAL CONNECTION

If you and another person share a structural connection, you both are members of a common group. You may be siblings, workers at the same organization, or fans of the same music. Belonging to the same group often confers an automatic degree of affiliation.

There are practical ways to strengthen your structural connections with another negotiator. You can find links that already exist or build new links as colleagues.

Find Links with Others

As you find a structural connection with another, your disagreement no longer becomes the sole tie that keeps you working together. Other connections help bind you together, motivate joint work, and act as a safety net in the event that discussion gets tense.

Before you negotiate, investigate possible links between you and the other. You might discover structural connections by asking questions of colleagues who know the other, by requesting the other's curriculum vitae, or by searching for information about the other on the internet.

As you meet with the other person, you might initiate a sincere discussion about some of the links that connect you, such as:

- your age ("On days like this, retirement looks tempting.")

- your rank ("Does your boss keep you working all weekend like ours?")

- your family ("Do you have kids? How do you balance work and home life?")

- your background ("What a coincidence that both your parents and mine were born in Berlin!")

- your religious conviction ("Do you have any good recipes for [Passover, Easter, etc.]?")

- a common interest such as hiking, music, or chess ("I really like skiing, too. It might be fun to get our families together to go skiing over the winter holiday.")

You may also be linked through your role as business partners, colleagues, fellow employees, classmates, friends, acquaintances, or fellow alumni of a university. A short discussion on your structural connections can bond you. ("You went to that university? I did, too. What dorm were you in?")

Build New Links as Colleagues

After the Yugoslavian wars in the 1990s, some Serbian Members of Parliament (MPs) came to view political parties other than their own as adversaries. This was particularly harmful, given that the governing coalition comprised seventeen parties who needed to negotiate to get any work done. Dan was brought in to train the Serbian MPs in interest-based negotiation. After observing negative emotions on all sides, he asked the Serbian MPs, "What is your best advice on how to negotiate?" In a single sentence, one MP summed up the dynamic that made things so difficult: "We should deceive the other side before they deceive us!"

The very fact that two people—whatever their shared jobs and experiences may be—are now dealing with each other *as negotiators* puts each in a role that tends to focus their attention on something about which they disagree. It may be politics, it may be something else, but there is some difference between them. Each, almost automatically, tends to accept the idea that as negotiators they are adversaries. The structure of a negotiation is assumed to be adversarial. That assumption explains why many negotiations fail.

Regardless of prior connections between you and another, there are ways you can build a connection as colleagues.

From the outset, treat the other as a colleague. Do not let the assumed structure of a negotiation—or conventional wisdom about how negotiators are supposed to behave—deter you from being constructive. Some simple steps to build links include the following:

- *Arrange to meet in an informal social setting.* Before important negotiations between the South African government and the African National Congress (ANC), Roelf Meyer, the government negotiator, arranged to "drop in" for lunch at a friend's remote country house, knowing that Cyril Ramaphosa, his ANC counterpart, would be there for a fly-fishing weekend.

- *Introduce yourself informally, suggesting that they use your first name.* "Hello. I'm Sam Johnson. Please call me Sam. May I call you by your first name?"*

- *Sit side by side, if that is reasonably possible.* "Since we are going to be working together, let's sit together here at this table."

- *Refer to the importance of their interests.* "As I see it, any solution we come up with will have to take care of interests important to you as well as interests important to us. I understand fairly clearly the interests on our side. But I doubt if I understand your interests as well as I should. If you would like to do so, I would welcome your taking a few minutes to lay out what you consider to be important interests on your

---

*The core concerns may be universal human wants. Tactics to meet each concern, however, are often culturally specific. In a collectivistic culture, for example, it might be seen as an insult for a junior colleague meeting with a senior, older colleague to suggest that they address one another by first name. We will not raise cultural variations throughout the book, but do want the reader to note that some of the tactical advice may need to be culturally adapted.

side. I could then quickly review interests of ours that we think important. This might help us both be clear on the major interests that will have to be taken into account in any agreement we reach."

- *Emphasize the shared nature of the task you both face.* "We certainly face a real challenge in coming up with something both our bosses can be happy with! Let's jot down your concerns and mine and go forward from there."

- *Avoid dominating the conversation.* "Before going any further, I think I should stop and ask for your ideas and your advice on how we can best proceed."

Make yourself indebted to the other. Benjamin Franklin suggested that doing a favor can help build a link between you and another. Rather than doing a favor for other people, however, he suggested that you let them do a favor for you. Borrow a book or otherwise ask them for a small favor that is easy to grant. You become indebted to the other person, and that person feels both generous and connected.

Plan joint activities. Engaging with your counterpart in a constructive task can build a structural link between you as colleagues or friends. Ask yourself, "What activity might I organize to build a link between us?" For example, political tensions between two countries can be reduced if someone organizes joint economic-development activities or student-exchange programs.

In most negotiations, you could invite relevant parties to join you for a brainstorming session to nominate ideas to deal with the differences you face. You might shift the meeting to a less formal location, change the seating arrangement so that everyone sits around a circular table, or lighten the mood with an icebreaker such as having each participant share a story from childhood. Or you might invite members of the other team and yours to eat together, to go out for drinks, or to attend a sporting event.

Exclude with care. Structural links that you build can easily be destroyed if the other person feels left out. Feeling excluded from team activities—whether a meeting, a conversation over coffee, or a questionnaire to colleagues about office space—can have a more powerful emotional consequence than many people realize. One day, during a coaching session with Dan, a high-level government official described the bitter resentment her colleague felt when he received no invitation to an important interdepartmental meeting. He had expected to be included in the meeting and felt alienated from the organization and the organizers. In retaliation, he apparently found a legitimate way to withhold several million dollars' worth of funds from the department that had organized the meeting. Not until six months later were the funds finally made available.

Exclusion from a meeting may seem trivial—but not for the person being excluded. As you plan your next meeting, whether lunch with colleagues at the local cafeteria or a meeting of key negotiating parties, remember to ask yourself if there is anyone who might be sensitive to being excluded. Take a moment to decide whether you want to invite them to participate. What are the benefits of inclusion? Possible costs of exclusion? One minute of thought can save you hours of grief. Even if you decide not to invite them, think about whether you could at least touch base with them to explain the reason, so they are not surprised and put in the position of hearing it from someone else.

REDUCING PERSONAL DISTANCE

Having explored how to build *structural* connections, we turn to the other aspect of affiliation—*personal* connections. These are the personal ties that make us feel closer or more distant from each other. Without such ties, one or both of us may question the other's honesty, fail to listen carefully, or as Roger recalls, even cancel a meeting:

In the early 1990s, some colleagues and I were invited to South Africa to give negotiation workshops for President DeKlerk's all-white cabinet in the capital city of Pretoria and for the

African National Congress (ANC) in Johannesburg. As we finished the workshop for the cabinet, the team got a message that the ANC had canceled the workshop that had been planned for the following week.

My colleagues and I went to Johannesburg and met with Cyril Ramaphosa, the ANC's Secretary General, and some of his colleagues. After some discussion, the ANC workshop was rescheduled and conducted.

On the day following the workshop, Ramaphosa took us to lunch. By that time, I knew Cyril well enough to ask, "Why on earth did you cancel the workshop that we had scheduled?"

"Because no one knew you," he replied.

"But," I said, "you knew all about me. In fact, if I remember correctly, you once wrote me at Harvard asking if I could get you a fellowship at the Center for International Affairs."

"I knew all *about* you," Cyril replied. "But I had never heard your voice. I had never seen your eyes. I had never touched you." He paused, smiled, and shook his head slightly. "I didn't know who you were."

For most people in the world, a human being is not simply a résumé or curriculum vitae. Getting to know someone as a person and being able to connect on a human level is often critical to forging a good working relationship. In even the simplest negotiation, personal ties between two negotiators can be crucial.

Connecting at a Personal Level

The degree of affiliation that one feels toward another tends to change, sometimes gradually and sometimes quickly. Without taking the time to become consciously aware of our personal distance from one another, we might not recognize that we are moving closer together or further apart.

For example, two siblings may fail to agree about whether to move their mother into a nursing home. Their dispute distances them. Without taking a step back and asking themselves how to improve their personal connection, they may overlook their potential to support one another as they watch their mother's health decline.

The optimal emotional distance between negotiators can be compared to the physical distance between porcupines trying to keep warm on a cold night. They huddle together, but do not want to be so close that they are being pricked by each other's quills. How emotionally close we feel to each other is often indicated by how physically close we behave, with hugs and kisses demonstrating emotional closeness and a chilly nod of the head or a brisk handshake revealing greater emotional distance. Understanding the physical signals of emotional distance can help you gauge the degree of affiliation between you and another; it can also warn you when you are in danger of overstepping the other's personal boundaries and getting too close for comfort.

Here are four tactics to help you connect with others at a personal level:

1. *Meet in person rather than via phone, computer, or e-mail.* Personal distance is better reduced by face-to-face conversation than through e-mail, letters, or the telephone. Once you get to know someone in person, it is easier to avoid stereotyping that person or misattributing ideas to them. Whether a negotiation involves Israelis and Palestinians, labor and management, or a landlord and tenant, face-to-face negotiation helps to humanize each of the parties and provides a greater depth of context. When people meet you in your office, you may want to avoid having your desk become a barrier. Former Secretary of State Dean Acheson regularly got up from behind his desk and moved to a chair near that of his guest. Roger has his desk facing bookshelves on the wall so that he can easily swivel his chair and greet a visitor who is promptly invited to sit nearby. Without a desk between you, it can be easier to build a personal connection.

After you have gotten to know someone face-to-face, affiliation can be further built without every subsequent meeting having to be in person. You have acquired a sense of each other as a person, which makes it easier to understand the other's tone of voice over the phone or the meaning of their words in a letter.

However, if a difference arises, it is often more efficient to work through your problems face-to-face rather than through a volley of e-mails. By dealing with problems in person, you reduce the danger of miscommunication. Each of you is able to convey your feelings through body language, tone of voice, and the content of your message. During a face-to-face meeting a person's voice can raise or lower to help indicate the extent of their feelings; there is no "volume control" on an e-mail.

2. *Discuss things you care about.* A second way to build a personal connection is to talk about things that you find personally important. We all know safe subjects, like traffic or the weather, where we won't offend others or reveal too much of ourselves. Conversations with the least risk, however, tend to be those that also offer the least benefit in terms of reducing personal distance.

Talking about personal concerns is likely to feel more revealing—with more sense of intrusiveness and vulnerability—and yet at the same time offer the greatest opportunity to forge a sense of closeness. Affiliation-enhancing topics are likely to include family issues, financial concerns, emotional reactions to a topic at hand, self-doubts about one's career, and ethical dilemmas.

On any such subject, a good way to open the conversation is to ask for advice. "I've been having a terrible time getting my colleagues to show up on time for a meeting. Do you have any suggestions? How do you deal with that?" Sharing your mistakes, weaknesses, and bad habits can also bring you and others emotionally closer.

Setting boundaries of confidentiality can make affiliation-enhancing discussions less risky. Before getting advice from another negotiator about how to deal with a problem at home or work, you might say, "I'd like to get your advice on a personal issue. Would you mind not sharing this conversation with others?" Or, after a personal discussion, you might say, "I'd appreciate it if you would keep this conversation between us."

Table 6 outlines some topics that can be used to build closer affiliation. It also suggests some "safer" topics that can be used to create greater emotional space if a conversation begins to feel awkward

TABLE 6

TOPICS THAT AFFECT AFFILIATION

Affiliation-Enhancing Subjects That Reduce Emotional Distance	Safe Conversation Subjects That Maintain Emotional Distance
Family	Weather
Personal concerns, plans	Some good restaurants
Children, siblings, or parents	Traffic
Personal opinions about politics	Favorite TV programs
Subjects away from the job (stories, personal philosophy, etc.)	Narrow "job" subjects
Soliciting advice (e.g., disciplining children, issues with spouse)	Automobiles
Sharing ambivalence and uncertainty	Saying nothing

or if you sense that you are in danger of crossing uncomfortable boundaries for yourself or another.

If feelings are too open and raw to discuss, acknowledge that fact. Religious leaders, for example, can communicate to warring groups that wounds are so deep that things are difficult to talk about now, which is natural and to be expected. Similarly, after the 2001 terrorist attacks on the World Trade Center, some psychologists encouraged people silenced by the shock of the situation to voice their emotional experience, even if only to say, "I'm at a loss for words." Such an acknowledgment strengthens affiliation, because people reveal their vulnerability. Rather than saying nothing, they open up and express their emotional experience, even if that experience is not so well defined as to be categorized with specific emotion words.

3. Consider giving space to bring you closer. A third tactic to build a personal connection is to allow others—and yourself—plenty of space. You need not damage the sense of affiliation in order to provide greater freedom. You can request space while remaining friendly. A Scottish couple once greeted their weekend houseguests with a cordial "Welcome" followed by "We are reading. What would you like to do?"

To build affiliation you need not share your deepest secrets. The purpose of affiliating with another negotiator is to humanize each of you, not necessarily to make new friends or heal your every family problem. You want to create enough of a personal connection that you increasingly trust one another and can deal with problems jointly and effectively.

If efforts to build affiliation appear to bring you or others "too close for comfort," consider backing off. You may have gone too far. We all have times when we want greater personal distance between us and others. We want time to ourselves, time to relax, time to think, time to be alone. If a conversation becomes too heavy, intimate, close, or personal for comfort, one can always change the conversation to a "safe subject," or take a break and do something else.

To build affiliation with someone whom you do not totally trust, you can limit the type of information you share. Imagine you have a close colleague who has a number of wonderful qualities, but who gossips about office politics. In this situation, it makes sense to refrain from telling him about office issues that you don't want other colleagues to hear. Still, you may decide to build affiliation by confiding in him about your own marital issues, information you are confident he will keep private.

4. *Keep in contact.* A final way to strengthen a personal connection is to check in occasionally with the other person, regardless of whether they are on "your side" or work for another organization. Affiliation is not static. It changes over time. Just as most personal relationships need to be nurtured, affiliation often requires regular maintenance. You can't just ignore your spouse and expect you both to continue to feel as strongly affiliated as you have in the past. To maintain a sense of affiliation, personal attention is critical. You might invite a member of your team to lunch, ask about their welfare, or inquire about their children.

Making It Easier to Build a Personal Connection

We may see the value in building a personal connection, yet fear doing so. Without a basis for trust, we may worry that the other side will mislead us. And even if we trust individuals on the other side, our colleagues and constituents may criticize us.

Three ways to make it easier to build a personal connection between sides are to hold private meetings, to reshape the public's image of a conflict, and to organize subcommittees to focus on specific issues.

Roger used some of these tactics in a contentious labor-management negotiation. He worked with the vice president for labor relations of a large American corporation who was trying to improve his working relationship with the head of the union. Both the union and the company saw their relationship as totally adversarial. Negotiations extended for weeks and weeks over wages, benefits, job security, and a host of other issues. Each side was angry, frustrated, and agitated. They dug their feet in the ground with firm demands and refused to budge to the demands of the other side. In fact, adversarial relations were so entrenched that this corporation had a specially designed Negotiation Room where labor and management met. A long wooden table stretched down the length of the room, lined with about twenty-five chairs on each side. Another fifty chairs were placed behind for support staff. Each side's negotiators sat across from the other, lined up like troops ready for battle.

Roger recalls thinking how to improve the affiliation between the two groups:

> My first inclination was to change the location of the meeting. Down the hall from the Negotiation Room was a conference room with a big round table at which everyone could sit side by side. I took the name cards of participants from each side and placed them alternately in front of chairs at this round table. Union representatives walked into the conference room, saw their name cards next to management name cards, and became

concerned. They approached me and said, "What's going on? Is this a trick? We want to sit next to our own team. If we don't go back to the other room, we'll walk out." Trust was so tenuous between these groups that everyone ended up back at the long table and accomplished nothing.

Yet given the tensions, both the union and management were interested in further consultation. I realized that personal, face-to-face interaction can help reduce the personal distance between adversaries. I invited the vice president and the head of the union to meet in my office at the Harvard Law School on an informal, unofficial basis to consider jointly what they might do toward bridging the structural divide between management and union.

As soon as the two men sat down, they started right away chatting with each other in the warmest and most genial manner that anyone might hope to see.

I reached into my desk drawer for my camera, hoping to record their smiles and looking forward to using such a photo to remind the two men at some future time of their personal rapport and cordiality.

On seeing the camera, both men immediately and strongly objected to my taking a photograph. Their shared concern was how such a photograph might look to their constituents. Both the top management of the corporation and members of the union viewed these two men as tough adversaries, ready to fight vigorously over any issue. Each feared that a photograph of them meeting privately together in a genial fashion could cause irreparable damage in the eyes of their constituents. Seeing such a photograph, top officials of the corporation might conclude that their labor-relations man was "in bed" with the union and could no longer be trusted to represent the corporation zealously in battle with "the enemy." The union president worried that such a photograph might seriously damage him in the eyes of union members, who might fear that their leader was secretly undercutting their position by building personal friendships with management.

The remainder of the meeting was productive but less eventful. I facilitated a joint brainstorming session on how the groups might settle some of their most divisive issues. The leaders brainstormed ways to help satisfy the underlying interests of each group. That year, no strike took place.

Hold private, unofficial meetings. In reflecting on Roger's intervention, it is clear that he recognized the importance of building personal connections between negotiators. He tried to build a context that was conducive to collaboration. His first attempt—moving the negotiators to a circular table—was unsuccessful. But he persisted. In the neutral terrain of Roger's office, the leaders met in an informal capacity. This context made it easy for the leaders to talk congenially and to discuss how to proceed.

Reshape the public's image of the conflict. Strong personal connections may not be enough to secure a collaborative relationship between negotiators. Although the union and management representatives had surprisingly good rapport in the privacy of Roger's office, they each maintained the public image of enemies. Each leader felt that he could not risk disclosing to constituents how close and comfortable he felt toward the other side without being viewed by his own constituents as a traitor to his cause. Yet Roger and both leaders realized that good relations between the two groups would enhance *each* group's ability to deal with current problems and future ones.

In some circumstances, leaders would be wise to demonstrate to the public that they are working together collaboratively on the problems that divide them. They might have a picture taken of them sitting side by side and working together on a joint problem.* Or they might coauthor a newspaper article or cocreate and distribute an e-mail message describing their intent to solve issues jointly.

Organize subcommittees to focus on specific issues. Reshaping their public image was unattractive to the union and management

---

*For example, see page 193 for a photograph of President Jamil Mahuad of Ecuador and President Alberto Fujimori of Peru as they work side by side to deal with an international border dispute.

leaders, who each feared that disclosing their personal connection would risk alienating constituents. In such circumstances, action might be taken to reduce the structural divide between groups. Subcommittees could be established on benefits, wages, job security, and other divisive issues. Each subcommittee could include a handful of representatives from both labor and management who would jointly brainstorm creative ways to deal with the focal issue of their group. The actual meetings would be private, and no substantive commitments would be made. Without feeling pressured to make binding commitments, participants would be structurally linked as joint brainstormers working on a shared problem. Over time, the work of these committees could help reduce the structural divide and make recommendations that would ease collaborative decision making.

Additionally, the leaders might rename the process by which they negotiate. *Collective bargaining* is a common name for the approach labor and management take to deal with differences between them. The assumption of positional bargaining is embedded in the word *bargaining*, which implies that the negotiation is an adversarial process of give and take. "We won't increase benefits unless you reduce demands for vacation hours." A simple change in the name to *interest-based negotiation*, or perhaps to *joint problem solving*, might emphasize the fact that the affiliation between negotiators does not need to be adversarial.

PROTECTING YOURSELF FROM BEING MANIPULATED BY AFFILIATION

To this point in the chapter, we have advocated that you build strong affiliations. Yet the stronger your affiliation with someone, the more likely your gut feelings will tell you to say yes to their requests. That may put you in a vulnerable position.

Wise decisions involve both your head and your gut. Each can serve as a good source for fresh ideas. Each can also serve as an excellent screening device to help you winnow out bad ideas and select the best. Before committing, consult both your head and your gut feelings.

Check a Proposal with Your Head

Strong affiliation can lead us to make bad decisions. A colleague may use peer pressure to influence us to do something. Teenagers use this tactic to pressure friends into drinking or smoking cigarettes. "Everyone else is smoking. Here. Try one." Similarly, someone with whom you are negotiating may use their affiliation with you to pressure you into committing to an agreement.

> As your longtime friend and colleague, I haven't asked for much. But now I ask you to say yes.

You feel the emotional pressure. And the proposed deal may be fine. In fact, it may be pretty good for you. But before you rely on your personal ties and emotional affiliation, stop. Check out that deal with your head. In fact, you may want to have in mind (or on hand) a sentence or two of preparation for just such pressure:

> I am not holding out a promise that I will be persuaded. But since you ask me, I will look at it again with an open mind and get back to you in the morning.

Committing to a poor decision is bad for you and often for the other party as well. If you were misled into buying a car that does not fit your family's needs, you are likely to feel buyer's regret. The car is not as good as you had hoped. You may feel angry at yourself for being "suckered" into buying that car. From the dealer's perspective, the situation is hardly more promising. The dealer may lose future business as you describe your buyer's regret to others and worsen the dealer's reputation.

Before committing to a decision, check it out with your rational thinking—with your head. If you are looking into buying a new car, first locate and check out some basic information about the models you like: What does *Consumer Reports* say about their safety, gas mileage, durability, and warranties? What sales prices are quoted on the Internet for different models? What is your BATNA—your Best Alternative To Negotiated Agreement? If you don't reach agreement with this dealer, where are you going to go, and what kind of car are you going to get at what price? And what are the costs of waiting for a few weeks to buy?

Check Also with Your Gut Feelings

There is no need to be overly suspicious of everyone with whom you interact. In fact, becoming highly suspicious of others will almost certainly reduce your ability to gain the negotiating power that comes through affiliation. Nevertheless, you do want to guard yourself. Before making an important decision, rely not only on your reasoning mind but also on your feelings.

Wherever a possible decision came from—a friend, an ad, or a TV commercial—your gut feelings can offer you a lot of helpful information as you decide. This is likely to be true whether you are thinking of buying a new car, taking a new job, firing somebody, or taking on a new associate. *And* you often can learn a lot by getting in touch with just how your body feels when thinking about such important decisions. Consulting others can be a big help, but you can also learn a lot by asking yourself how you feel. Relax, take your time, and start considering such questions as:

- How am I feeling about becoming committed to this decision?

  (Scared? Happy? Confident? [*long pause*] Feel your feelings.)

- If I said no, how would I be feeling tomorrow morning?

  (Relieved? Disappointed? Frustrated? [*long pause*] Close your eyes; check your gut.)

- If I now said yes, how would I be feeling tomorrow morning? (Does such a decision feel right? Why?)

The distinction between what you *think* in your head and what you *feel* in your gut is useful, but it is not always as clear cut as our language suggests. For example, if you conclude that for you to do something would not *feel* right, are you looking only to your own personal emotional reaction to that conduct, or are you reacting to what you anticipate might be the critical views of a friend or colleague? The more closely you are affiliated with someone, the greater the risk that your feelings about an action you might take (for example, clothes you might wear) would not be your own internal emotional reaction, intuition, or gut feelings but rather your guess of how a person with whom you are closely affiliated might feel. When you are checking with your gut or your intuition to learn how something would feel to you, you may need to be careful not to substitute someone else's presumed feelings for your own. By using your head and your gut, you protect yourself from being manipulated by affiliation, and you improve the quality of your decision.

SUMMARY

With enhanced affiliation, working together becomes easier and more productive. There are two qualities to affiliation:

- *Structural connections:* These are links you have with someone else based upon your common membership in a group. You can strengthen structural connections by finding links that you have in common with someone or by creating new links.

- *Personal connections:* These are the personal ties that bond you with another. By talking about personal matters, you can reduce the personal distance between you. But make sure to give people plenty of space, too.

CHAPTER 5

Respect Autonomy

Expand Yours (and Don't Impinge upon Theirs)

S top reading this book. *(Now!)*

Although you may want to put this book down anyway, you almost certainly object to being told. And rightly so. By *telling* you what to do, we have impinged upon your autonomy—your freedom to make and affect decisions.

Each of us wants an appropriate degree of autonomy. If a police officer walks up to you right now and handcuffs you, the handcuffs restrict the use of your hands. The handcuffs impinge upon your autonomy, even if there is nothing you want to do with your hands right now.

The greater the autonomy *we* exercise, the greater the risk that our actions will be perceived by another person as impinging on *their* autonomy. A case in point involves "Elizabeth," a seasoned corporate lawyer, who recalls a negotiation that she thought was going to be a "simple, consensual buyout":

I arrived at O'Hare Airport accompanied by two legal associates for our first meeting with John, the lawyer for the other side. He was alone. And he appeared surprised and apparently quite upset to discover that I had brought two young lawyers with me.

"I understood," he said, "that this was going to be a preliminary meeting between just the two of us to get acquainted and to make plans based on the suggested agenda I sent you. We're clearly facing a long negotiation."

"But," I said, "my two associates are the ones who have prepared our preliminary draft of a final agreement. I do want them here for our discussion."

"Draft of a final agreement!" he exclaimed. "That seems awfully pushy. You bring your team with you, and they bring a draft agreement? All this before you and I even meet? In any event, my wife is expecting the two of us for dinner tonight, and we will be able to talk then."

"Dinner? Sorry, I didn't know that and have made other plans."

"Then I'll call my wife and tell her that dinner is off," he said. "Let me invite you to meet with me now, one-on-one, in the two-person Airport Conference Room B that I reserved just upstairs. We can then consider whether or not to expand that meeting to include your two colleagues."

"Sounds like a plan," I responded.

"Well, of course," he said, "I don't know whether a larger room is even available now."

Obviously, this negotiation did not get off to a good start. Apparently, neither negotiator had thought about who could appropriately make what decisions without involving the other. Even in trivial logistical matters, emotions can quickly get stirred. Usually this is not because someone made a *wrong* decision, but because a decision was made without consulting the other person. As a negotiator you should be ready for trouble if the decision you made that affects the other can be responded to with:

"I did not agree to that!"

"I was not consulted!"

"I was not even informed!"

We easily get offended when others limit our scope of autonomy beyond what we think is appropriate. They may pressure us to acquiesce to their demand: "That's our final offer—take it or leave it." They may try to limit our thinking: "Don't even *think* about walking out on this deal." Or they may discourage us from feeling certain emotions: "You shouldn't feel sad about losing the deal. Just get over it."

OBSTACLES TO USING AUTONOMY WISELY

If we fail to manage autonomy well, it can stimulate negative emotions in us and in others. Ultimately, those emotions can harm the outcome of our negotiation. Two obstacles stand in the way.

We Unduly Limit Our Own Autonomy

In everyday life, most of us have the autonomy to decorate our office as we would like, to decide what we want to eat for lunch, or to choose our own bedtime. In a negotiation, however, we often are blind to the many ways we can exercise our autonomy. We may limit our own autonomy because we feel powerless to affect change or to influence others. If we are not the final decision maker, for example, what kind of impact can we have on the negotiation? As you will see, there is power in *not* having authority.

We Impinge upon Their Autonomy

When our autonomy bumps up against the autonomy of another, we may feel as though we are walking through a minefield without a map. A misstep on autonomy can derail an entire negotiation. If the other side's autonomy feels impinged upon, they are more likely to reduce their trust in us, to reject our ideas whether useful or not, and to invest little effort to implement "our" agreement.

To stimulate positive emotions, then, you will need:

- to expand your own autonomy
- to avoid impinging on the other person's autonomy.

EXPAND YOUR AUTONOMY

The power of autonomy primarily rests in our ability to affect decisions. Many of us wrongly assume that without the ability to authorize a decision, we are powerless. And if others lack such authority, we view *them* as powerless and not worth dealing with. Why negotiate with the junior associate who showed up at the meeting if he is not authorized to make commitments? If we are representing a client, why go into a meeting with the other side if we have no authority to make decisions? We may worry that others will see us or our ideas as "weak."

Do not unduly limit your autonomy. There are powerful ways you can affect a decision even if you do not have decision-making authority. You can make a recommendation to someone, invent options before deciding, and conduct joint brainstorming.

Make a Recommendation

No one but you limits your ability to make a recommendation to someone. If you are disappointed at the way your company is dealing with a problem, develop some useful ideas. Do not constrain your ability to think creatively about problems and about ways to address them. Consider:

- What is the problem that I want to address?

- Who do I want to influence?

- What recommendation can I make?

- How can I get my recommendation to the decision maker?

Invent Options Before Deciding

The ability to affect a negotiation need not depend upon having the authority to make a binding decision. By brainstorming, you can invent possible decisions that might later be made. This is best done if you can talk freely without having to worry that something you say might amount to a commitment. You and others can step "outside the box" of conventional thinking. The fact that you have no authority to make a binding decision gives you enhanced autonomy to generate new ideas and fresh possibilities. Freed from the risk that something you say might limit your authority, you need not worry about locking yourself or a client into a poor decision.

Roger recalls how he expanded his autonomy during the Iran hostage situation:

In the fall of 1979, the United States Embassy in Teheran was seized. Most of the diplomats and other members of the American staff were held hostage for many months. In the spring of 1980, President Carter tried to rescue them by helicopter. The attempt failed.

Shortly thereafter, White House Counsel Lloyd Cutler phoned me and asked me to see what I could do about the hostages. Cutler made it clear that I had no authority to make a binding commitment of any kind. Cutler would be available twenty-four hours a day through the White House switchboard. He obviously recognized that a government official who tried to brainstorm with Iranians would likely be heard as disclosing what the U.S. government was willing to do. Whatever was said by an official could then be interpreted as a bargaining proposal, to which the Iranians could be expected to ask for more.

As a freewheeling professor working through a small, nonprofit, nongovernmental organization, I saw my purpose as trying to generate a package that I might recommend to both sides.

Through a student in Iran, I got in touch by telephone with the Ayatollah Beheshti, head of the Islamic Republican Party, who spoke English fairly well. Beheshti had apparently learned something about me. His manner was surprisingly genial. The conversation was roughly as follows:

ROGER: "What are Iran's interests? What do you want?"

BEHESHTI: "I'll tell you what we *don't* want. We don't want the New York courts to have anything to do with our financial claims."

ROGER: "Who do you want to decide any financial dispute? The Iranian courts?"

BEHESHTI, laughing: "No, not that. How about arbitration at the Hague?"

ROGER: "Do you think Iran will accept arbitration?"

BEHESHTI: "Right now, I will commit Iran to accept arbitration at the Hague. Will you commit the United States to do so?"

ROGER: "As I told you, I have no authority of any kind to commit the United States. If we can work something out, I am prepared to recommend it to the White House. What else does Iran want?"

Beheshti outlined a number of issues that would have been difficult subjects for a U.S. diplomat to discuss without the usual rhetoric. In talking with me, however, the real interests beneath the positions came out.

BEHESHTI: "Sanctions must be ended."

ROGER: "Ouch. Give me some good arguments that I can use with the U.S. government to recommend ending sanctions."

BEHESHTI: "First, we have been punished enough."

ROGER: "Well. President Carter could say that, but there is no clear standard for how much punishment would be 'enough' in this case. I will need more arguments."

BEHESHTI: "Well, to continue sanctions risks destabilizing the whole area."

ROGER: "Please explain that point. Why is that so?"

BEHESHTI: "Don't you understand? Doesn't your government understand?"

ROGER: "I don't know what the United States understands, but *I* don't understand. Why do sanctions risk destabilizing the region?"

BEHESHTI: "To import or export items contrary to the sanctions, officials on one or both sides of the border have to be bribed. And the longer bribery of officials goes on, the more we and our neighboring governments lose control over the boundary areas."

ROGER: "That's a good argument. Give me one more."

BEHESHTI: "Let me think. Oh, if the United States fails to end sanctions when the hostages are released, it will never have a better excuse for doing so."

ROGER: "I like that point. I will certainly use it with the White House."

By making clear that while he had access to officials in the White House, he had no authority to commit the government of the United States to anything, Roger's autonomy to explore interests and generate a possible political package was expanded. He could talk freely without the risk that his remarks would be taken as a commitment nor understood as revealing some hidden position of what the government might be willing to do. By playing an unofficial role, he was better able to generate the substance of a possible agreement than he would have been if he had had the authority to make a binding decision. At the same time, his unofficial role made it easier for Beheshti to talk without making government-to-government commitments.

Separating inventing from deciding can be useful in almost any negotiation. If Kate and Steve are going to buy a new car for him, they may decide to have Steve go alone to look over various cars, sit in them, and drive one or two that he likes best.

Steve realizes, however, that a dealer may try to pressure him into buying a car. The dealer may want to run a credit check, give him a sales pitch, or find out how much he is willing to spend. Wisely, Steve makes clear to the sales personnel that he does not want to make a final deal without his wife. He and his wife will have to decide together. He expands his autonomy to explore cars without excess pressure, and buying a car turns from being stressful to being fun.

Now Steve and Kate move from exploration of options toward commitment. Steve informs Kate about the cars he liked. He checks the Internet on the cost of these new cars to the dealership, while she calls a few other dealerships to find out their sale prices. They weigh the pros and cons of each car and of the dealer's treatment toward Steve. At the least, a good relationship with the dealer is important if there are any car troubles.

They then go off to the nearest dealer who is offering the desired car at a low price. Here Kate and Steve explore a package deal including extras, price, and delivery date. If they agree with the dealer on a reasonable package, they exercise their autonomy to make a firm commitment—and buy a car.

Conduct Joint Brainstorming

A third way to expand autonomy is to conduct joint brainstorming. In this process, you and the other party explore options without deciding, refine those options, and then decide among them. Whether you are negotiating a business transaction or a government policy, if you want to give joint brainstorming a try, follow the five steps on Table 7.

Even in emotionally heated conflicts such as divorce, joint brainstorming can help. For a couple with children, a divorce is likely to involve a mix of difficult questions and strong emotions. Perhaps the clearest example is when a husband and wife who have children are negotiating custody issues in an amicable divorce. The autonomy of each spouse is very likely to bump up against the autonomy of the other. A checklist of open issues includes decisions about visitation times, household rules, medical and dental needs, religious upbringing, and which school to attend.

TABLE 7

FIVE STEPS FOR JOINT BRAINSTORMING

1. Decide who should participate.

- Select six to a dozen people with knowledge on the subject and differing points of view.
- Include some who have access to a decision maker.
- Invite each participant "in their personal capacity"—not as a representative.
- If participants hold strong views on the topic, consider getting a facilitator.

2. Explore interests.

- Participants on each "side" jointly draft their best estimate of the other side's interests.
- Each side shares their list and invites feedback and "corrections" from the other.

3. Invent options without commitment.

- Make clear: "Nothing said at this stage is a commitment."
- Each participant generates ideas that might satisfy important interests of everyone.
- Welcome wild ideas. (They might stimulate better ones.)
- List all ideas on a flip chart for everyone to see.

4. Refine options

- Everyone nominates ideas that might best meet the interests of all.
- The group selects a shorter list of options that deserve further consideration.
- The group sharpens those ideas into operational possibilities.
- They simplify each idea until the word "yes" is a sufficient and realistic response.

5. Decide what to do with the ideas.

- Nominate deciders to whom these options might be recommended.
- Enlist volunteers to convey ideas to deciders.
- If some participants are themselves deciders, ask their advice: "Is there something we could do that would make it easier for you to say yes?"

The underlying question—which of the divorcing parents has the autonomy to make decisions about their child—is likely to stir up strong emotions. The chance of ending up with a tolerable divorce for the parents and the child is likely to depend on the parents' spending enough time together, or perhaps with a mediator or facilitator, to conduct joint brainstorming.

Of course, the wife or husband can skip this complex brainstorming and simply go to court and request the terms of a divorce. A busy judge may use his or her autonomy to grant the request within a few minutes—often to the financial and emotional detriment of everyone, except perhaps the lawyers and the taxing authorities. The ex-spouses, their children, and their lawyers can now argue for years over issues that might have been settled more wisely and less expensively through joint brainstorming.

In other situations, members of some organization or group have little intrinsic authority or have left what they had at the door. During joint brainstorming, they may want to devise ways to communicate their recommendations to a particular decision maker. Participants may decide to write a memo, jointly or alone, or they may decide to share suggestions orally with decision makers.

Caveat: A Great Deal of Autonomy Can Be Overwhelming

Sometimes the problem is not that we lack autonomy, but rather that we feel overwhelmed by having too many choices and too many decisions to make. Viktor Kremenyuk, a Soviet expert on negotiation, was having lunch with Roger at a Cambridge restaurant. The waitress handed our Soviet colleague a long and complicated menu:

"Would you like to order?"

"Do you have a special? Fine. I'll take it."

"How would you like the meat? Medium, well done, or rare?"

"Medium is fine. Thank you."

Thinking that he had finished the task, Kremenyuk turned to conversation with Roger. The waitress then asked:

"How would you like the potatoes? Baked, mashed, or French fries?"

"Baked potato, please. Thank you." Again, he tried to resume the conversation with Roger.

"Do you want a salad?"

"Yes, thank you."

"What kind of salad—Caesar salad, Cobb salad, or the house salad?"

"House salad, please. Thank you."

"And what kind of dressing would you like on the salad."

"Whatever you have, thank you."

"Oil and vinegar? Russian dressing? Blue cheese?"

"Whatever you suggest, thank you!"

"Whatever you want."

"All right. The blue cheese. Now where were we, Roger?"

As the waitress walks away, Kremenyuk exclaims: "Being on per diem, I am paying for this meal. Even my friends wouldn't make me work so hard for my food. In Moscow, when I order the special, I get the special."

With autonomy, as with each of the other core concerns, we want to feel an *appropriate* degree of satisfaction. More autonomy is not always better. We can be overloaded with decisions to make.

DON'T IMPINGE UPON THEIR AUTONOMY

Too often, when we *do* have decision-making authority, we fail to include in the decision-making process those people who will be impacted by our decision. By excluding others, we risk impinging upon their autonomy—and having to deal with their consequent anger and resentment.

Negotiators are often wholly unaware of the emotional impact of their unilateral decisions. We would be taken aback if the other side simply announced, "Our next meeting will be in my office on Thursday at 10:00 A.M." They are focused on the merits of the decision and ignore the process by which that decision is made. The other side's office might in fact be the best place to hold a meeting. They may feel more confident and open in their own office; and for us it means we can leave whenever we want. What is upsetting is not the content of the decision but rather how it was reached. Were we included or excluded from the process? The answer to that question is likely to affect not only how we feel about the decision but also how we feel about working with the other person.

Consider the situation of Roger and his wife, Carrie, as they drove north to Vermont to attend a friend's birthday bash. As they set out, they stopped to buy flowers as a gift for their hosts. They bought two expensive plants. The cashier pointed out that there was a special bonus that day of a dozen roses at no charge with any purchase of $25 or more. Roger proposed that if she rang up the two plants as two separate sales, he could get two dozen free roses. She agreed, rang up the plants as two separate sales, and Roger got two dozen free roses.

He stayed to pay the florist for the plants as Carrie took the roses across the street. On her way to the car, she met by chance some good friends who helped her carry the flowers. When Roger joined them and offered to relieve the friend of the bunch of roses she held, he learned that his wife had given her a dozen of "his" roses. He smiled and said "Great," but felt irritated.

Back on the highway, Roger tried to figure out why he was so irritated by his wife's decision. It was perfectly reasonable to give the flowers to their friend. If consulted, he would almost certainly have thought it was a good idea. But he had not been consulted, and in his view the two dozen roses were clearly a result of his initiative and his work negotiating with the clerk. Carrie had unilaterally decided to give half of them away without considering that he might have had a plan for them himself.

Roger concluded that he was upset because his wife had taken action that impinged upon his autonomy. What happened to the roses, he believed, was for him to decide—or at the very least, to be consulted. Once he understood the source of his irritation, his anger dissipated.

If people can get emotionally upset over something that unimportant, it is easy to understand how a negotiator may become quite upset over any decision that has been unilaterally made by someone else. Such a decision might be about where to meet, when to start, what kind of sandwiches to order for lunch, or when to break for the day. Negative emotions may arise less over the content of the decision than over the fact that one negotiator chose to act unilaterally.

Always Consult Before Deciding

Our advice is to keep watching for ways that your behavior may impinge on the autonomy of others. The simplest remedy is to Always Consult Before Deciding—or ACBD for short. Carrie might have held off on giving the roses to their friend. When Roger arrived, she might discretely have asked him, "What do you think about giving a dozen roses to Liz?"

Consulting another before you make a decision has three important benefits. The other feels included in the decision-making process. You might learn something through the consultation. And you still maintain veto power. Consulting another does not give them the power to choose the outcome of the decision, but rather to provide input.

Consulting does have a drawback. Roger discussed the meaning of ACBD with his wife and suggested they try to Always Consult Before Deciding. A few days later, she said, "Do you know the trouble with ACBD? It means NGAD—Never Get Anything Done!"

She was right. There is a balance to be struck between too much unilateral deciding and too much time spent consulting. Some former students have adopted a revised motto that can safely be applied in all but the most urgent crises: Consider Consulting Before Deciding.

Invite Input from "Invisible" Stakeholders

Rarely are all stakeholders present at the negotiation table. Millions of constituents are affected by an economic agreement negotiated by two political leaders. Thousands of union members and administrators are influenced by the decisions of a dozen labor and management negotiators. A family of eight vacations at a location decided by the mother and father.

Trouble may brew if we fail to respect the autonomy of these invisible stakeholders. Without their "buy in," constituents may speak poorly of an organization, exert little effort to implement their small part of an agreement, or even try to sabotage it. American consumers may not buy merchandise from a company that has negotiated extremely cheap labor from a third world country. Union members may work halfheartedly if they fail to receive the salary increase they expected. Children may resent vacationing if they were not consulted about the place.

Although a decision may not have an immediate impact on someone's position, it can affect that person's life in important ways. An employee may sourly note, "I just took out a second mortgage on my house. If this company is falling apart, my job falls apart with it. Why didn't the corporate heads let me know in advance! And what am I going to say *today* to my subordinates worrying about the future of their jobs?" The anxiety and resentment of enough employees can produce an unmotivated workforce and, perhaps, a failed company.

Thus, it is a useful practice to respect the autonomy of these invisible stakeholders. It would be too overwhelming to negotiate with thousands of constituents or employees. It can even be overwhelming to negotiate a vacation with a houseful of children. You may be able to consult with them, however, and, in any event, you can usually inform them of decisions that are being considered.

Consulting with stakeholders. Ask stakeholders for their input on decisions that will be made. You might create a system where stakeholders can e-mail their suggestions to a central location, place recommendations in a suggestions box, or call in their ideas to a designated person. Or you might organize a consultation committee of stakeholders. For example, suppose the CEO of a nationwide pharmacy chain is negotiating new store policies with branch executives. Before deciding anything, the CEO might set up a consultation committee that includes a couple of cashiers, pharmacists, marketers, and managers of local stores. The CEO instructs the committee members to solicit from their colleagues input on key issues being negotiated, and then to report their findings to the consultation committee. Several of these committees could be formed across the country. A summary of the recommendations could be forwarded to the CEO.

With any system, it is unlikely that *everyone* will offer input. Yet you can create an atmosphere that promotes inclusion in decision making. People can feel that they have a voice in a matter, even if they do not have the final choice.

Informing stakeholders. You can respect the autonomy of stakeholders by informing them of decisions whenever possible. If appropriate, inform them of decisions you are in the process of making. If this is not feasible, inform them of decisions promptly after they are made.

For example, the pharmacy chain may need to modify their policies to comply with revised government regulations. Though the CEO of the corporation wisely consults with lawyers and top executives, there may not be enough time to form a consultation committee or to take into account suggestions from every employee. In this case, the CEO may want to change the policy and then, without delay, inform employees of the change and why it was necessary.

By consulting others, we can tailor our decision to satisfy their interests. And the mere act of keeping others informed of decisions can save governments, families, and companies from the perils of ignoring stakeholders' autonomy.

An example: The impact on employees of a merger. Too often top management ignores what is going to happen to the autonomy of their employees.

The chairmen of two companies met, were persuaded of the overall economic benefit that could result from a merger, and decided to go ahead. They jointly decided who would be chairman of the new enterprise, who would be the chief executive officer, how much each would be paid, how much money would change hands as one company bought the stock of the other, and what the name of the combined company would be. The merger was then announced to the press.

Most mergers fail, as did this one.

Although the chairmen had correctly estimated the potential economic benefit of combining the two companies, they had failed to take into account the emotionally charged issues generated by such a merger. Of course, they had the autonomy to explore those issues, to brainstorm options, and to take preemptive action. Yet they failed to use their autonomy wisely.

If the chairmen had consulted widely, they could have learned a lot. Autonomy was important at all levels of both organizations. The grades and pay scales of the two companies did not match. The two companies had markedly different internal cultures in terms of formality, dress codes, keeping office doors open or shut, and the use of first names. All these features raised issues of great importance to employees. About those issues and others, employees on both sides could have been consulted. Many could have been involved in the process of dealing with such differences. As it was, their autonomy and their emotions were ignored. The resentment of a great many employees over that merger led to its demise.

To Establish Decision-Making Guidelines, Use the I-C-N Bucket System

We are often at odds about the "right" amount of autonomy each of us should have in affecting and making a decision. The autonomy of a boss, a spouse, a partner, or a counterpart in negotiation can be protected by sorting decisions to be made into three "buckets." The three buckets are to *I*nform, to *C*onsult, or to *N*egotiate, or I-C-N for short.

Some years back, a partner in a small, Cambridge-based negotiation consulting firm was asked to take on the role of managing partner. The firm had a dozen partners and another dozen employees. Given the high number of partners, the question was soon raised about the managing partner's decision-making autonomy. What guidelines should the firm establish about the managing partner's authority to make decisions?

For a couple of weeks, the managing partner kept a record of the many decisions with which he was faced, and then he had a meeting of the partners. The managing partner ran through the kinds of decisions he and the firm had to make and the partners each held up one, two, or three fingers to indicate into which bucket a decision of that kind should go. What startled the partners was that there was almost no disagreement as to which issues fell into which bucket.

Bucket 1: *Inform.* These were thought of as small decisions that the managing partner could make on his own and then simply inform the rest of the organization. These were decisions like buying new furniture and hiring office staff.

Bucket 2: *Consult, then decide.* Into the second bucket went significant issues that the managing partner had authority to decide but only after consulting other partners. Just who he consulted was up to him, but he was expected to consult partners who were likely to have views on the subject. It might, for example, be a decision of the firm to take on a potentially unsavory client like a tobacco company. After deciding, he would promptly inform partners of the decision.

Bucket 3: *Negotiate joint agreement.* Into the third bucket went those big decisions where the managing partner had to negotiate and obtain agreement of a majority of the firm. All partners wanted to participate in "big decisions" such as making new partners or moving the firm's office to a new building.

The three buckets can come in handy for labor-management negotiators and others who work together over time and face similar decisions again and again. The process also helps those who work together to keep from stepping on each other's toes without being paralyzed by the need for constant consensus.

Even in an organization of only two people, such as a personal relationship, the bucket system can help with decisions ranging from handling money to making social plans. As Dan recalls:

I planned to surprise my wife by taking her to a French restaurant to celebrate our upcoming wedding anniversary. Saturday arrived, and I revealed my plans to Mia, who had a surprise for me. She had already planned a girls' night out with a few of her friends but had not informed me. We were both disappointed as plans for a romantic evening quickly crumbled.

We discussed ways to avoid this kind of grief in the future and decided to use the bucket system to answer a few key questions:

- On what days of the week can we make plans on our own? [bucket 1]
- On what days should we consult with the other before making plans? [bucket 2]
- On what days should we decide plans together? [bucket 3]

We decided to do as we each would like on weekdays, to consult before deciding on weeknight plans, and to negotiate weekend plans.

The bucket system also can be useful in dealing with money issues. For one member of a couple to make a unilateral decision to spend what the other considers a lot of money is almost certain to stir up emotions—usually negative. Dividing such financial issues into buckets can help. ("Let's neither of us buy anything that will cost more than $100 unless we both agree on it.") Brainstorming together in advance of buying big items can eliminate many of the most troublesome money issues. Yet, the simplest and most basic rule about protecting autonomy is probably CCBD—Consider Consulting Before Deciding.

BACK TO CHICAGO: WHAT TO DO WHEN AUTONOMY IS IMPINGED

Remember Elizabeth, the corporate lawyer who flew to Chicago to work out a routine business deal? We were introduced to her quandary at the beginning of this chapter. She found herself clashing more and more over autonomy with John, which created tension from the outset. What advice might we give her to deal more effectively with autonomy?

In the Moment

Elizabeth is doing her best to sustain a working relationship with John during this unexpectedly stressful interaction. She is listening to him rather than becoming sullen and quiet, walking off, or accusing him of being obstructive. She has disclosed the fact that she wants to include her two associates in the interaction and that she has alternative plans for the evening. Nevertheless, her interaction with John appears to be spinning out of control. They are both reacting to what the other is saying. Misunderstandings and distrust are piling up.

As a first step, Elizabeth can use autonomy to slow things down in her own mind. Before saying or doing anything else, she can pause and take a deep breath. She might consider excusing herself for a moment to go to the restroom, where she can spend a few minutes figuring out how to get this negotiation back on track.

Running down a checklist of core concerns, it will quickly become apparent that Elizabeth has impinged upon John's autonomy. She surprised him with her two associates, her dinner plans, and her draft of a final agreement. None of these decisions is "wrong," but Elizabeth seems to have stepped into decision-making areas that John feels are at least partially within the scope of his autonomy.

Elizabeth might consider apologizing for her role in the confusion and let John know that her intentions were good *and* that she recognizes the emotional impact of her impinging upon his autonomy:

> I'm sorry for any misunderstanding my actions have created. I was trying to be as helpful as I could. Still, I certainly should have communicated the fact that I was bringing my two associates and we had gone ahead with a preliminary draft agreement.

To move the negotiation forward, Elizabeth might ask: "How do you suggest we spend the rest of the day?"

She would be wise to listen carefully and to appreciate his ideas, communicating merit she finds in them. If he conveys no ideas, she might offer a possible agenda that respects his autonomy and hers:

> I'm not planning on signing any agreement today. I'm more in-terested in exploring possible options that might satisfy your in-terests and ours. So what if you read through this draft agreement and spot issues for us to talk about? We can add or subtract issues as you like. Then when we talk, we might invite my associates and yours if you want. By early afternoon, we can block out where to go from here. How does that sound?

She expands John's autonomy by suggesting that he can add or subtract issues as he likes. Rather than seeing the proposal as a final set of commitments, he can provide input into the shaping of an agreement. John's autonomy expands further as she suggests that he might invite some of his associates to the meeting. And by asking him "How does that sound?" she acknowledges that she wants to negoti-ate jointly the process of their interaction from this point forward.

In Hindsight

Now we come to the much easier question: With the luxury of hind-sight, what might she do differently to enlist positive emotions from the very start of her interaction with John?

Much of the confusion could have been alleviated by simply consulting John before flying to Chicago with two assistants. And it could have been wise to talk to him before preparing a draft agree-ment. A few days before traveling, Elizabeth might have called John and said:

> As you know, I'm only going to be in Chicago for one day. I'm trying to figure out how to make our time together most efficient.

Although none of us, I believe, is thinking of committing to an agreement on this trip, I thought that a rough draft of a possible agreement might help us get focused on key issues. I could ask two of my associates to prepare such a rough draft and send it to you. Or would you prefer to prepare such a first draft and get it to us?

Either way, before we meet we might better understand important issues that we would like to discuss.

Do you have associates working with you on this business deal? Might it be useful for us to involve one or two associates on each side at this first meeting?

In terms of the day, I was thinking we probably need all the time we can squeeze in. I'll be at the airport by 9:30 and can work as late as you want, though I wouldn't mind seeing some personal friends for dinner. What would work well for you?

Notice that by inviting John to put together the first draft, trust is likely to build between the two of them. He now has little reason to believe that Elizabeth has manipulative purposes for volunteering to shape a first draft. Whether or not he revises the draft agreement, it is clear that each of them will contribute to it.

Then there is the issue of her associates. John understandably felt surprised when she showed up with two associates. Here he stands alone to greet Elizabeth, and he discovers she has brought along a small entourage. He probably felt disempowered, and perhaps even manipulated, as though she were trying to intimidate him through a show of superior strength. It is true that Elizabeth has a right to bring along her associates. And it may even be true that they can advise her well during the negotiation. Yet prior to meeting John, she almost certainly should inform him of her plan to have them accompany her. In this way, Elizabeth preserves her own autonomy to bring associates and respects John's autonomy to prepare for her team's arrival. He might decide to bring one or two associates of his.

Whether or not John feels overpowered by the imbalance of team members, there are also practical issues at stake for him. If he is picking Elizabeth up in his sports car, there might not be room for two extra associates. Dinner reservations might need to be revised to include two additional people. All the other little details that he might have arranged to make the day comfortable and productive would now have to be revised. Simply informing him beforehand could save a lot of emotional trouble and enlist a lot of helpful emotions.

SUMMARY

We all want an appropriate degree of autonomy. When someone impinges upon it—whether intentionally or not—we tend to experience negative emotions. When it is respected, we tend to feel engaged. As you negotiate, take the initiative:

- *Expand your autonomy.* Whatever your authority, you can always make a recommendation or suggest inventing options before deciding. Joint brainstorming is a practical process for you to invent options for mutual benefit.

- *Avoid impinging upon the other person's autonomy.* You can consult before deciding, whether with a colleague or with invisible stakeholders. To clarify decision-making authority, you might work with colleagues to implement the I-C-N bucket system: On which issues should you decide alone? Consult before deciding? Negotiate? By respecting people's core concern for autonomy, you can stimulate positive emotions in them and in yourself.

CHAPTER 6

Acknowledge Status

Recognize High Standing Wherever Deserved

A middle-aged man was admitted to the hospital. He complained of chest pains. The doctor determined that he was at only mild risk for a heart attack. He was placed on a basic care floor with heart monitor attached to him. A nurse kept an eye on the monitor throughout the night.

In the morning, a young doctor walked into the room, glanced over the patient's medical history, and talked with him for a few minutes. The nurse said to the doctor, "I noticed some unusual heart rhythms around midnight. You might consider sending him to the intensive care unit."

"The patient reports he feels better this morning," the doctor responded. "And I have no reason to send him down there over a few unusual rhythms."

"But doctor, it would take time for . . ."

"How many patients with heart problems have *you* treated?" snapped the doctor. "I've examined the patient. I've made my diagnosis. And I've decided on the treatment plan. Now get the forms completed."

The nurse quieted. She felt foolish for offering information that appeared to be of little use, and she felt angry at the doctor for demeaning her suggestion. As the doctor walked away, she recalled the patient's more severe chest pain that radiated up his arm in the middle of the night, but decided that there was no use in telling the doctor. He already had made up his mind.

Ultimately, the doctor stuck to his judgment. The nurse said no more. Hours later, the patient experienced a massive cardiac arrest. It took ten minutes for the appropriate resuscitation team to arrive in the ward. The patient survived but became dependent on life support.

How did this brief interaction result in such a poor outcome? The core concern of *status* has a lot to do with it. Status refers to our standing in comparison to the standing of others. If our status is demeaned, we may feel embarrassed, ashamed, or frustrated, and we may act unwisely. In the hospital example, the nurse withheld additional information, and the doctor failed to inquire further about the nurse's observations. The result: The patient nearly died of a heart attack.

STATUS CAN ENHANCE OUR ESTEEM AND INFLUENCE

It is no wonder that people want status. As the hospital story illustrates, there are valuable consequences to having it. Status elevates both our self-esteem and the esteem with which others view us. Everyone wants to feel like "someone"—a force to be reckoned with, a voice worth heeding, a person to know. Whether it is because of our training, accomplishments, family background, job, or position in the organization, we are likely to enjoy having a lofty status that is recognized by others and by ourselves.

High status also adds weight to our words and deeds. We can use our high status to influence others. An employee is more likely to be amenable to working over the weekend if that request comes not from a midlevel manager but at the personal request of the chief executive officer. As expressed by the motto of a former brokerage firm: "When E. F. Hutton talks, people listen."

THERE IS NO NEED TO COMPETE OVER STATUS

Negotiators often compete for higher status as though there were one single dimension of status. If one person is high in status, then the other is assumed to be lower. We may see ourselves as superior to a colleague in terms of importance, rank, or approval. Yet that colleague may disagree, thinking that he or she outranks us.

Negotiators may even use tricks to obtain higher status. They may invite you to meet in their office, have you wait ten minutes for them while they finish up with another "important" client, and then welcome you into their office where you sit on a low chair looking up at them.

Competing for status tends to induce negative emotions. People who feel put down become resentful and less cooperative. Treating others as inferior tends to make them less able to think creatively or work collaboratively.

This chapter provides you with an alternative to competing over status. The first section reminds you to pay attention to people's *social status* in order to gauge the extent of courtesy that they expect of you. The second section suggests that whether or not others have higher social status, each of you has some area of higher *particular status* based upon expertise or experience. You can refer to that particular status to raise someone else's self-esteem and to influence your own. The third section offers suggestions on how you can raise your status—and how it can be lowered by you or others.

SOCIAL STATUS:
TREAT EVERY NEGOTIATOR WITH RESPECT

The level to which we are regarded as someone important or famous is our social status. This is a single, all-purpose measure of standing for everyone within a geographic area, such as within a neighborhood, an organization, a city, a country, or the world. The lofty social status of a rock singer may stretch across the globe, whereas the high social status of a sheriff may stop at the county line.

At a global level, society "tells" us who is important and who is not. At the top of the social order are VIPs—very important people—of all kinds: royalty, presidents, movie stars, prime ministers, and people of great wealth, achievement, or fame. At the bottom of the social order are the disenfranchised: the poor, the unemployed, and the homeless. The rest of us fall somewhere in between.

At an organizational level, co-workers tend to treat one another differently depending upon where each is situated on the corporate ladder. Employees may treat their chief executive officer like a movie star, while those low on the rung may struggle for basic recognition.

Even in one-on-one negotiations, people are often sensitive to their social status. Negotiators tend to evaluate where they stand socially in comparison to their counterparts, sometimes jockeying for higher social standing. They might mention the university from which they graduated, an important event they attended last week, or the major promotion they received. They may try to outdo one another in terms of their relative social importance or treat the issue as unimportant.

Become Aware of Social Status

Throughout a negotiation, people may share specific information about how they view their social status in order to indicate how they expect to be treated. Those who are high in social status—such as the president of an organization or an ambassador—may expect to be treated with particular deference. This is not always true, but it is helpful to be alert for signs of such expectations. With a little bit of preparation and some careful listening, you can learn a lot about where people think they stand in terms of their social status.

Listen closely to the way they describe themselves. Does a negotiator refer to her course at Yale? Does she talk about the important people she had dinner with last week? Does she hint at her senior position in a high-powered firm?

Language often provides the clearest clue as to how people rank themselves and others. Pay attention to what level of formality makes people feel appreciated and comfortable. Some want to be addressed by their first name and some by title, such as Doctor, Lieutenant, or Professor.

In virtually all cultures, the words we use can express our views of a person's social status. For example, a speaker can demonstrate greater respect by referring to "you" in French as *vous* rather than more informally as *tu*. In some cultures it can be offensive for a low-level negotiator to address a high-level official by his or her first name. (If in doubt, it is usually safer to start with a formal address and let the other invite you to be more casual.)

You may set an informal tone by introducing yourself by your first name and asking how another prefers to be addressed. Professors often request that their graduate students address them using their professorial title and last name. One student reported the elation he felt on the day that his mentor said to him, "Please, don't call me Professor Smith. Call me John." This shift in formality signaled a shift in the type of relationship between them. In the eyes of the professor, the student's status had been raised through hard work and good relations.

If you have a higher social status than another, there is a chance that he or she will have an interest in vicariously acquiring some social status by working with you. Any such desire for personal association would tend to encourage a deepening emotional commitment to have the negotiation succeed so that a more lasting relationship could be forged. Working with a skilled negotiator or a famous person can give somebody a boost in social status.

Your social status often depends upon the values within your team, organization, or group. In some Internet companies, for example, seniority is not as socially valued as youthfulness. An executive with fifty years of corporate business experience may not be as highly valued in such a rapidly evolving field as an enthusiastic twenty-three-year-old right out of college, bursting with creativity and knowledge of the latest computer innovations.

Be Courteous to Everyone

In general, when we think about other people's status, we first focus on social status. If the other is a VIP, we may automatically treat them with courtesy. *And,* to maximize the benefits of positive emotions, we recommend treating *every* negotiator with courtesy—whatever his or her social status. Every negotiator holds high status as a human being worthy of dignity and respect.

A little courtesy can go a long way. While consulting for a Fortune 500 company, Dan learned that an administrative assistant to the chief executive officer of the organization was being treated poorly by two or three of the employees. They ignored her, treated her with little respect, and did not invite her to some work-related parties at their homes. A few years into her job, the administrative assistant married the CEO. All of a sudden, everyone was coming to her house for parties. Now that she had full access to the key decision maker in the organization, everyone wanted to be her "best friend." Not surprisingly, she gave partiality to those employees who had respected her all along.

Courtesy is more than just saying please or thank you. It involves honest respect for the person with whom you are interacting. The administrative assistant to the CEO told Dan that though many people now treated her with courtesy, she easily could sense who sincerely respected her and who was simply trying to use her.

PARTICULAR STATUS: ACKNOWLEDGE EACH PERSON'S HIGH STANDING WHEREVER DESERVED

Your relative standing is based not only on the perceptions of society but also on how you are rated—by yourself or others—within some narrowly defined substantive field. Whether or not you have a high social status, you may have high standing in terms of your particular expertise, experience, or education. We call your standing in each field *particular status.* You may have skills in auto mechanics, home repair, or business networking. You may have the ability to play a musical instrument beautifully, write persuasively, or analyze ethical issues wisely. You may be knowledgeable in a variety of fields pertinent to the subject of a negotiation.

Fortunately, there are hundreds of different fields in which your status can be measured. Everyone has a comparatively high status in some particular field—and a comparatively low status in others. An unemployed carpenter may know a great deal about a well-constructed home. A skilled doctor may know little about maintaining administrative records. There are an infinite number of particular fields in which a person can hold a high status. And there is at least one particular area in which your status outranks that of many others. By the same token, another negotiator is almost certain to have at least one particular status that exceeds yours.

Look for Each Person's Areas of Particular Status

The better you understand how others see their own status, the more equipped you will be to enlist their positive emotions. You will know how they view themselves and what they deem to be important parts of their identity.

A brief list of areas in which they may have a high particular status could include:

- education
- computer skills
- business experience
- technical skills
- "big picture thinking"
- cooking ability
- connections
- moral standing
- social skills
- life experience
- emotional insight

- professional skills of different kinds
- strength
- athletic ability

Visible areas of high social status—fame, fortune, and fashion—often overshadow the less glamorous, but often more important, fields where status is critical in a negotiation. There are an unlimited number of fields in which others may hold high status. Two questions can help reveal fields of particular status.

Is either of you an expert on substantive issues? Substantive issues are the content of your negotiation. Your negotiation may be about a new car, a plot of land, or a raise in salary. Even before meeting the other party, familiarize yourself with the subject matter of your negotiation. Find out information on the Internet. Ask friends. Call up stores that sell similar items and get their advice on what to watch out for in your upcoming negotiation.

The other party's substantive expertise can benefit each of you. For example, imagine that you are negotiating the purchase of your neighbor's used computer. By asking him questions about the computer, you can learn a lot. He informs you that he worked as a computer programmer for ten years. This makes it clear that he has particular status as a computer specialist. You inquire about the computer's memory capacity, speed, and how the computer compares with newer models. Your curiosity rewards his concern for status, enlisting positive emotions in him. He is in the satisfying role of being the one with superior knowledge helping the two of you develop a common understanding of the substance of the negotiation.

Trusting the seller to educate you completely could leave you open to being exploited. It is always wise for you to conduct a substantial amount of preparation. You will certainly want to learn some things before making a binding commitment. You may decide to consult an impartial expert such as a computer technician at your workplace. Nevertheless, after learning from the seller, you now know more about the subject and about him than you did before you met. And you have built some personal rapport as you talked together about a subject he knows well.

Is either of you an expert on the process of negotiation? An important issue in any negotiation is how to structure the discussion. An effective process, for example, often involves exploring each other's interests and brainstorming options before making binding commitments. The more knowledge you have about how to structure the negotiation, the higher your particular status as a negotiation expert. If either of you has particular expertise in terms of how to structure the negotiation effectively, discuss those ideas. Ask the other party for advice. (See chapter 9 for suggestions on establishing a good negotiation process.)

We are not giving general advice to trust others. Trusting others is a matter of case-by-case risk. As you decide how much you want to trust others, however, remember that there are costs in being overly suspicious, just as there are costs in being overly trusting.

Recognize Their High Status, Then Yours

The fact that there are multiple fields of particular status makes your job easier. Rather than having to compete with the other negotiator over who is the alpha negotiator, each of you can have superior status in some particular field of expertise or experience. With a little creativity, you will find areas in which your status trumps theirs and areas where their status trumps yours.

Consider an example. The economics department at an Ivy League university was interested in promoting their department's research through op-ed articles, presentations, and interviews. The department hired "George," an editor, to assist their most distinguished economics professor in writing op-ed pieces for newspapers. This professor had a reputation as being both brilliant and arrogant. George immediately faced the challenge: How do I acknowledge the professor's status without putting myself down? George did not want to work daily with someone who would belittle him.

After some creative thinking, he had an idea. At his first meeting with the professor, he said:

It's a pleasure to be working with you. I feel that we each have something of value to enhance our collaboration. You have expertise in economics. As I see it, you are basically the leader in the field. My expertise is in having a good sense of what the "average reader" of an op-ed will understand.

In this way, George established the professor's expertise in economics, as well as his own expertise in assessing the extent to which an average reader could comprehend the op-ed. He turned his inexperience with economics into an advantage and did so in a way that did not demean the status of the professor. The two were able to work effectively together without the fear of competing for status as to who was smarter, more knowledgeable about economics, or a better writer.

Asking advice is a powerful way to acknowledge the high status of another person while not diminishing your own status. As Dan recalls, this can work in even the most unexpected situation:

After a corporate negotiation training in Pittsburgh, I walked to a neighborhood restaurant to eat a late dinner and review the day's events. A waitress informed me that there were no more tables available, but that I could order dinner at the bar. I spotted an empty barstool, sat down, and jotted down some notes.

I heard a voice to the left of me yell, "Who does this guy think he is?!"

I ignored the comment and continued writing. No one could be talking about me. I'm minding my own business. I don't know anyone here. Then curiosity, or perhaps anxiety, got the best of me. I looked to my left. Two stocky men stared back at me. The one sitting to my left watched the situation with avid interest. He was egging on the other, a bearded man with an angry red face. I felt the eyes of a few of their bar friends staring at me.

The situation did not improve on its own. The moment my

eyes met the eyes of the bearded man, he stepped closer to me and said: "Do you realize you're dealing with *danger?*"

I paused for a moment and said, "Yes." Clearly he was right about that point. And I wanted to let him know. If I said no, it was apparent that I would have threatened his status as "tough guy." With all of his friends watching, it was in my interest for him not to worry about losing social status.

The bearded man continued to stare at me, as though he were preparing to punch me. My mind was churning with thoughts about how to deal with this situation. I wanted to defuse the situation. But how?

Thoughts raced through my head about what to do: Can I just walk out? No. He'll follow me. Can I ask the bartender for help? But he's not nearby right now. Can I call the police? I don't know where the phone is. Should I just tell him to back off? But he won't.

I felt stuck. I wanted to let him prove to his friends that he was a tough guy, and without punching me. If I appeared "small" to him, he might see me as an easy victim. How could I respect his status while not demeaning mine?

Suddenly it occurred to me. I could ask his advice on a subject on which he holds high status. I asked, "What advice do you have for someone on how to deal well with danger?"

The expression on the bearded man's face shifted from anger to pride. He was now in the high-status role of advising *me* on how to deal with *him*. He stood there for a moment without talking. I didn't move. Without another word, he raised his head in pride, looked at me as though he had privileged information, and sat back down at his bar stool. Two seats away from me, he was no longer concerned with me. He turned his attention back to his friends.

In this example, Dan was cautious not to demean the social status of the bearded man. He realized that countering with threats of his own would increase the personal stakes for the bearded man,

whose friends eagerly watched the interaction. Dan's goal was to reduce tensions, not escalate them. He paused to ask himself, "How
can I respect his status while not demeaning mine?" He recognized
that the issue between them was "dealing with danger." By asking
advice about danger, Dan shifted the bearded man's role from ag-
gressor to the comparably high-status role of advisor. Suddenly, the
bearded man was being recognized for an area in which his particular status was high: on dealing with danger.

Take Pleasure in Your Areas of Status

No matter how old or experienced we get, there are times when we
all have to turn to others to shore up a flagging sense of self-esteem.
Some years ago, Roger's assistant came into his office with a handful
of letters, every one of them criticizing something that he had written
or done. He turned to his assistant and asked, "Doesn't anyone like
what I do?"

"Oh yes," she replied. "Most of the letters are just fan mail,
which I acknowledge and file. But these letters are problems that you
have to deal with."

Roger told her to reverse the practice. "Bring *me* the fan mail.
And *you* suggest what I should do about these problems."

It is much more emotionally rewarding to read praise than criticism. Roger, in fact, can spend hours responding to critics, but his revised practice reduced the risk of being overwhelmed by the negative.

Appreciate your areas of high status. Be confident about what
you have to contribute to the negotiation—from your professional
expertise to your personal qualities. Give yourself a boost when you
need it by recalling close friends or family who appreciate you. Keep
a picture of someone supportive on your wall or in your wallet.
When your status is demeaned, imagine how someone who cares
about you might praise you for your analytical ability, your patience,
or your sense of humor. Remember, you can gain status in every interaction if you learn from the experience.

After a tough negotiation, take pleasure in your achievement as you review what you have learned from the experience. Take pride in what status you have accumulated in the substantive fields in which you have gained knowledge and in such social status as you may have acquired. Savor what you have done and recharge by indulging in activities where your status is affirmed, whether playing a sport with a colleague or cooking with friends.

KNOW THE LIMITS OF STATUS

If a person has a higher status than you, it is important to give weight to their opinion where deserved. At the same time, you want to guard against being unduly influenced if they overstep the bounds of their high status.

Give Weight to Opinions Where Deserved

Appreciate a person's particular status where relevant to the negotiation and worthy of special weight. Consider what happens if you have a toothache. You tell a good friend, who tells you it's probably nothing. But your neighbor, a reputable and competent dentist, examines your tooth and warns you that it needs extracting immediately. You would be wise to treat the dentist's opinion with special weight, because it is based on an area in which he holds particular status.

Those high and low in the formal hierarchy of an organization each have areas of particular status deserving of weight. This was certainly true in the case of a teachers' union and school administration negotiating a policy for evaluating teachers. Should evaluations happen every year? Every other year? Should it be based upon the results of standardized testing of students, or upon observations by the principal?

Dan worked with the two parties before their formal negotiation began. At first, leaders on each side saw the other as an impediment to getting their own interests met. But they came to realize that each side held important areas of status. The teachers had specialized knowledge about the pros and cons of gathering evaluation information from parents, students, fellow teachers, or standardized tests.

And administrators had specialized knowledge of state policies and district requirements. Rather than compete over who was better positioned to develop an evaluation policy, each expressed appreciation of the other's special knowledge. Together, they drafted a proposal that drew upon each side's particular status. Appreciation of the other's status enlisted positive emotions and reinforced their motivation to work together.

Sometimes, however, the other may say or do something that inappropriately lowers your status. In such a situation, it may be important that your areas of high status be understood by others so that you do not feel put down or disempowered. To do this, you can clarify your role.

Consider the situation of a young female lawyer as she met with one of the senior partners of another firm. She arrived a few minutes early at the meeting room and found a senior partner for one of the other parties sitting at a head table and looking over his notes. Without looking up he said, "Miss, would you get me a cup of coffee from over there? I like it black with no cream or sugar."

The young lawyer flushed. Her head flooded with questions. "Should I simply inform him that I'm not a secretary? Should I educate him that nowadays many lawyers are women? Should I just get him a cup of coffee and have him learn later of his mistake?" She did not want to embarrass him if he was indeed mistaken; nor did she want to appear to be weak or a pushover. She responded:

> I'm sorry I failed to introduce myself. [*She demonstrates graciousness by assuming the senior partner unintentionally mistook her for the secretary.*] I'm Sarah Jones, the lawyer for Smyth, Wilcox, and Adams. [*She clarifies her role.*] Since we're both here early, maybe we could talk about the issue we'll be working on this morning. [*She establishes her professional behavior within that role.*] In any event, I'll first get coffee for us. Help yourself to the doughnuts over there. And if you get one for yourself, please get one for me. [*She indicates that they share a status as colleagues working together on issues.*]

The young lawyer took responsibility for the apparently mistaken identity, introduced herself, and graciously assured him that she would get coffee for both of them. Rather than try to score points, she demonstrated her professionalism and colleagueship by suggesting that they use the fact that both were there early to share ideas about the upcoming discussion. And she indicated their shared status by requesting that he might get them doughnuts while she gets them coffee.

The big point is that whether an emotional issue relates to social status or particular status, it is rarely if ever a good idea to try to raise oneself up by putting another down. Clarify for others your role and play it professionally. Rather than competing over status, respect the status of others and communicate yours.

Beware of Status Spillover

There is a constant risk that the opinions of a person who has high status, either socially or in some substantive area, will be given undeserved weight on a subject to which their status is irrelevant. We call this *status spillover,* and it is something to watch out for. Deference is due only where it is deserved. Those with high social status, based on their fame as movie stars, for example, have sometimes used that status to market their opinions on everything from gun control to salad dressing.

Of course, it is possible for actors and socialites to become an expert in some unrelated substantive area—but be careful. Don't let their status in one area persuade you of the validity of their opinions in an area unrelated to the basis of their fame. An actor on television promoting a particular medicine and wearing a white coat and stethoscope around his neck may look like a doctor, but don't be fooled. He's no doctor. No matter how skilled the actor, the views he expresses should not be taken as those of a doctor who has had years of substantive medical training and experience that earned him a high level of particular status.

Although negotiators with high social status may expect special courtesy, their social status does *not* mean that their opinions on matters under negotiation automatically deserve special weight. A woman of high social status might greatly admire a diamond necklace at Cartier's or a hundred acres of prime ocean-front real estate. She may suggest that with her high social status she should be able to buy the necklace or the real estate at what *she* considers to be a fair price. No. A wise seller would not lower the fair market price because of the opinion of one who simply holds high social status. Her lofty status may deserve special courtesy. But high social status adds no special weight to her opinion on an issue of value.

Status spillover is a real risk in a negotiation. Consider the challenge of "Melissa," a young woman searching for a house to buy. She sees one she likes, and her real estate agent pressures her to buy it today. "It'll be gone by tomorrow if you don't act quickly," he says. She worries that she might not find a good mortgage rate by the end of the day and fears committing to the house without financial clarity.

Her agent reassures her that rates are the lowest ever. But Melissa wonders, "Is he being honest, or is he interested in the 5 percent commission he will make on the sale?" The real estate agent may know a lot about houses, but he is not a mortgage broker. The young woman would be wise to watch out for status spillover.

To protect yourself from status spillover, start by recognizing the areas of status that others *do* have. They will be more likely to listen to you if you acknowledge their particular status. Keep it honest. False flattery will not go far and may backfire. Melissa may let her real estate agent know that she appreciates his competence in finding a house that matches her desires.

Consider seeking a second opinion. It is not an insult to have a policy of seeking a second opinion on important matters, whether the original recommendation comes from your boss, your lawyer, your doctor, or your spouse. Melissa might say, "I have a standard practice of getting a second opinion. Perhaps you know the names of two or three mortgage brokers or banks that you might suggest that I consult about a mortgage?"

Another way to protect yourself from status spillover is to ask the person about the pros and cons of your other choices. Medical doctors, for example, usually recognize that a decision is up to the patient, but many fail to outline the costs and benefits of other choices.

Imagine that a relative of yours asks a doctor about how to deal with some possible cancer cells in his throat. The doctor responds, "I recommend surgery to remove the cancer. But it's not my choice. It's yours. What do you want to do?"

Do not let your respect for the high status of the doctor prevent you from exploring your options. Rather than take the doctor's recommendation at face value, your relative might ask the doctor about other possibilities. What are they? To postpone surgery for six months? To have a less invasive procedure? To try a new medication? Whether it is health or real estate, negotiation is about getting your interests satisfied.

Finally, recognize that you always hold higher status than others in one respect: You are the world's best expert on your feelings, your interests, your needs, and your particular situation. This inherent particular status can often protect you from status spillover—if you recognize its value. A car dealer may pressure you to buy a car, saying, "I've worked with lots of families. Most come back and tell me how much they love this particular car. I think you should buy it today before prices go up."

You might respond, "Thank you. I'll certainly consider it. Now I would appreciate your helping me explore other options that are available given my interests. We want a car that is safe, that is big enough for camping equipment, and that gets good mileage. What are some other possibilities?"

By acknowledging another negotiator's particular status, you can shift their perception of themselves from that of an adversary pressing for a sale to that of a high-status expert working with you to help you formulate a decision that will best meet interests on which you are the expert.

REMEMBER: STATUS CAN ALWAYS BE RAISED—
OR LOWERED

Many people assume that one's status is fixed. This assumption is perhaps based on the concept of royal status that depended on the blood of kings and queens: One is born into an upper class. In most cases, a person's status is not determined by birth. Reputations are made, not born. It is within your power as an individual to raise your status by effort and achievement.

By educating yourself, you can improve your status in the substantive areas of a negotiation. Before you negotiate with your manager about realigning what you see as her unfair work expectations, you might sit down with a human resources representative to learn your organization's work policies. You can use the Internet to study up on business transactions, legal processes, car facts, and any subject that can help enhance your particular status in the negotiation. The power to improve your status in a substantive field rests largely with you. If your social status is hampered by bad habits of yours or a lack of interpersonal skills, you can take a class or hire a coach to help you manage your emotions more effectively, be more assertive, or listen more carefully to others.

Raising one's status—and lowering it—is not just a question of fate. How we act makes a big difference. When Roger was a first year law student, Professor James Landis was Dean of the Harvard Law School and taught Roger and more than a hundred classmates their first year course in Contracts. Roger considered Dean Landis—and still does—as the best teacher he had at Harvard Law School. Dean Landis later carelessly failed to file federal income tax returns for several years. The law finally caught up with him. He was tried, convicted, sentenced to prison, and disbarred. For better or for worse, one's status is not predetermined but can—and will—be changed by what we do and fail to do.

BACK TO THE HOSPITAL

Let us now revisit the hospital case that opened this chapter. Tension built between the nurse and doctor, and the patient experienced a massive heart attack. What went wrong, and what advice might we give to the nurse, the doctor, and the hospital administration?

Advice for the Nurse

The interaction began on a positive note. The nurse communicated to the doctor her observations from the prior evening. Once the doctor questioned her medical expertise ("How many patients with heart problems have *you* treated?"), she accommodated to his assessment of the situation. But because she felt angry and useless, she decided not to provide the doctor with additional information.

Although the hospital culture may provide doctors with high *social status,* the nurse lost sight of the fact that she had several important areas of *particular status* in which she outranked the doctor. Rather than blindly accommodate to his perspective, she quickly might have self-reflected on her areas of high particular status. For example, she had worked at the hospital for more than twenty years, giving her particular status in terms of experience recognizing patient symptoms. And she spent significant time talking with this specific patient, watching his heart monitor, and examining his medical records, giving her particular status in terms of personalized knowledge of the patient's physical and mental health.

She could have recognized that these areas of status are important—and extremely relevant—to the specific needs of the patient. She acquired information that needed to be communicated, and she had an obligation within her role to communicate it. She should not have let the doctor's social status intimidate her into withholding relevant information. She might have said, "Doctor, before you make your diagnosis, I have important information to be considered. We can't dismiss it."

To reduce her anger, she might have tried to understand how things looked from the doctor's perspective. It is likely that his high social status covered up his own insecurity as a young doctor, new to the ward, and fresh out of medical school. This awareness could have prevented his potential insecurities from stirring hers. Rather than feeling anger toward the doctor, she could have invoked compassion for his personal insecurities.

Advice for the Doctor

The doctor's job is not easy. He is expected to be in ten places at once, and patients and staff look to him to make wise and informed decisions. Because the doctor is new to the hospital, it is likely that he wants to establish a reputation as competent and respected. And the fact that he is nearly half the age of many of the doctors and nurses with whom he works does not make things easier.

The doctor met with the patient for a few minutes and reviewed his medical history. The doctor concluded that the patient's heart condition did not merit serious attention. He became annoyed when the nurse suggested that he consider sending the patient to the intensive care unit. He probably felt demeaned by this comment, as though the nurse were trying to demonstrate her superior competence on such matters.

Yet he erred in assuming that his high social status made him "all-knowing." This is a classic case of status spillover. Rather than seeing the nurse as holding high particular status about the patient's heart condition, he acted superior in all regards. He failed to listen to the nurse or to ask good questions. And he incorrectly assumed he knew all the important facts about the patient's health. Understandably, the doctor also had a lot of work too. But the thirty seconds it would have taken to listen to the nurse could have prevented the patient's heart attack.

In the future, the doctor would be wise to recognize that his job requires him to work *with* the nurses. They are not competing for status but are collaborators in helping patients. Instead of seeing a nurse's role as subservient, he can recognize that she holds important areas of particular status. There is no need to demean her. In fact, by appreciating her perspective, he can build rapport, improve communication, and enhance patient treatment.

Advice for Hospital Administrators

At a broader level, a hierarchy of social status may be so embedded in the hospital system that a larger intervention is needed. A small group of hospital staff—perhaps a combination of administrators, doctors, nurses, and others—might develop and promote new hospital policy that keeps work patient-focused. Such policy might help hospital staff recognize that the most important interest in the hospital is shared: improving patient welfare. By joining together and recognizing each other's areas of particular status, the medical staff can accomplish more than they otherwise would by upstaging one another.

SUMMARY

You need not struggle for medals or accolades to prove that you are a good negotiator and a worthy person. While your social status may be inferior to that of a movie star or a CEO, you have many areas of particular status that trump theirs. It may take a little time to figure out your strengths, but you have them. We all do. With a little self-preparation, you can identify your areas of high *social* and *particular* status and work to improve or develop new ones so that you can approach your negotiations with a sense of confidence.

Since every person has multiple areas of high status, there is no need to compete with others over status. Appreciate the high status of others where relevant and deserved and feel proud of your own areas of expertise and achievement. While it takes chutzpah to strive for approval, it takes just as much chutzpah to be satisfied with who you are and to value what you bring to a negotiation. If you truly appreciate your own status, you need not worry about what others think of you. In turn, you can acknowledge the status of others without cost. And treating others with appropriate respect often makes them respect you.

CHAPTER 7

Choose a Fulfilling Role

and Select the Activities Within It

W e all have a concern with having a role that is personally fulfilling. We do not want to spend our days and nights playing phony roles or trying to be someone whom we are not. In a negotiation, playing an unfulfilling role can lead to resentment, anger, or frustration.

This was the situation faced by "Ryan," who sought advice from Dan on how to negotiate his upcoming performance review. He explained that his most recent review went poorly:

> I walked into my boss's office for my performance review. I was nervous. My yearly bonus rides on a successful review, and my ego cannot handle too much abuse.
>
> "Have a seat," said my boss. He pointed to the chair on the other side of his desk.
>
> I tried to assess whether my boss was in a good or bad mood. That information would tell me a lot about whether this meeting would be easy or painful. His face looked somber and serious. Not good.
>
> My boss said, "Obviously, this meeting is to talk about

your performance evaluation. Generally speaking, your performance over the past twelve months has been acceptable. There are some aspects that need improvement, but let's start with the good news. . . ."

He went over a list of things I had done well this past year; but, to be honest, I wasn't listening. I was worrying about what areas would "need improvement."

Then he said that we were going to move on to the topic of improvement. That's when I sat up in my seat. And that's when things got tense.

"For starters," he said, "you need better follow through. You forgot to write up that memo last month for our biggest client. We're lucky they stayed on board."

"But that memo was not my responsibility," I said. "And there are at least ten other memos that I sent out ahead of schedule."

"Fine," he said. "But that's what I saw."

I sat quietly. My heart was beating rapidly. I tried to stop myself from arguing. I did not want to give my boss the satisfaction of rattling my nerves, but I also wanted him to have an accurate impression of who I am.

"You need better availability," he continued. "I know you have a family. But there is work to be done. We have customers to serve. If you have to pick up the kids, bring your cell phone."

"I try my hardest to be available," I said, "but I can't be available twenty-four hours a day."

"Fine. But that's what I've observed."

My boss continued to point out mistakes I had made, and I tried not to take his critique personally. But I was not successful. I rebutted many of his criticisms with little effect. Thirty minutes later, I walked out of his office emotionally exhausted, angry, and with no indication that I would receive a bonus.

As Ryan experienced during his performance evaluation, roles are not always as fulfilling as they could be. He felt like a victim to his boss's judgment, and he played the uncomfortable role of defender of his own behavior. He barely listened to his boss's positive feedback. Not surprisingly, the performance evaluation went poorly. Ryan received virtually no constructive feedback, he lost motivation to work hard, and his boss reinforced his own role not as mentor but as dictator.

This does not have to happen. You can shape your roles to feel comfortable and "right" for you and others. This chapter shows you how. We begin by describing the core concern for a fulfilling role. Next, we suggest ways to make your *conventional role*—whether as a business executive, psychologist, or stay at home parent—more fulfilling. We close by advising you on how to make your *temporary roles*—such as problem solver, listener, or facilitator—more fulfilling.

A FULFILLING ROLE HAS THREE KEY QUALITIES

We play roles all the time. Yet rarely are those roles as fulfilling as they could be. Whether at work or at home, a role may feel pointless, meaningless, or insincere. To build a more fulfilling role, we need to understand its three key qualities.

- *It has a clear purpose.* Engaging in a fulfilling role is not a futile exercise. There is a clear purpose, whether to improve society or to relax by taking a walk. A clear purpose provides an overarching framework to your behavior.

- *It is personally meaningful.* Only you can know with certainty what is personally meaningful to you. Often, a role may be meaningful in relation to what you do. Engaging in the role of parent may fulfill your desire to raise a child. Or, if you enjoy problem solving, a job as an engineer might be fulfilling. A meaningful role incorporates your skills, interests, values, and beliefs into the task at hand.

  Meaning is found not only in what you do but also in how you perceive a situation. Your role can be fulfilling in relation to how you "make meaning" of a situation. A dress manufacturer may hate his work obligations but nevertheless find his role meaningful because it allows him to support his family.

- *It is not a pretense.* When we talk of *playing a role,* it may sound as though each of us is an actor pretending to be someone. But the core concern that each of us has with *role* is not a matter of who you should pretend to be, but rather with the role that defines who you really are. In this life—the life you are living, not a life you are pretending to live—you want to have a fulfilling role.

In one sense, of course, you are on stage. You are assuming a role and playing yourself in that role. But that role is not a pretense. It is for keeps. It is really you, being yourself, not pretending to be someone else.

Roger and Dan each find themselves playing the many roles of professor, husband, writer, colleague, landowner, and negotiator. In each of those roles they are themselves, not some character in a play. They seek to shape each role so that they find themselves not as someone of whom they would be ashamed but rather somebody of whom they can be proud. They want to be pleased not with their acting ability but with the reality of what they do and have done. They want to make their roles fulfilling.

MAKE YOUR CONVENTIONAL ROLES MORE FULFILLING

Conventional roles are commonly accepted roles that people play within an organization or community. You might play the role of "vice president" of a company or "parent" within your family. Table 8 lists common conventional roles.

Become Aware of Your Conventional Roles

You can avoid unnecessary conflict by becoming aware of the roles guiding your behavior. In some cases, two of your own roles may bump up against one another. For example, the demands of a parent with a newborn child may compete with the demands of remaining the "star employee" at work.

TABLE 8

CONVENTIONAL ROLES

Academic	Nurse
Actor	Parent
Analyst	Politician
Artist	Real estate agent
Chef	Recruiter
Child	Scientist
Client	Secretary
Customer	Seller
Doctor	Sibling
Executive	Student
Fashion designer	Teacher
Finance officer	Technician
Grandparent	Travel agent
Lawyer	Truck driver
Manager	Writer

In other cases, you may disagree with someone else about who should play what role. You may be negotiating on behalf of a client, a trade union, or some other entity with particular interests. Yet you also have your own interests. Becoming aware of your roles is the first step in managing a role conflict.

Consider the situation of "Eileen," an executive at a business in which the operations pollute a water supply. She starts to think, "What kind of person *am I*? Am I a bad person if I work for a polluter?" She feels guilty for working for an industry that goes against her own environmental beliefs and ashamed that she is not living up to her own moral standards.

If Eileen fails to think about the conflict between her roles as business executive and environmentalist, she risks getting angry at her subordinates, colleagues, or boss for "no apparent reason." She will be, in essence, acting out internal tension without a clear purpose in mind.

On the other hand, with awareness, Eileen can decide carefully what to do. She may decide to talk to colleagues and her boss about ways to reduce the damaging by-products of their industrial operations. She may decide to leave the company. Or she may decide that

because the company lives up to industry standards, there is no conflict with her own beliefs. Whatever her decision, she actively clarifies
the conflicting roles that cause her stress. As a result, she can take action to make her roles more fulfilling.

Shape Your Role to Include Fulfilling Activities

You can shape virtually any role to make it more fulfilling for you. In
order to do so, turn your attention away from a role's job label and
toward the set of activities associated with it.

Every role has a job label and a set of activities. A *job label* is a
shorthand way of describing what, in general, you "do." Just as people have a first and last name to identify themselves, roles often have
a name to identify them, such as personal injury lawyer or child psychologist.

A role is more than just a job label. Every role has a corresponding *set of activities* that is expected of us. A company might advertise a new executive position by specifying the job label and
associated set of activities:

> **WANTED: CHIEF OPERATING EXECUTIVE.** [That's the job label.]
> Responsibilities include guiding the mission of the organization,
> overseeing executives who direct each department's activities, and
> reporting to the Board of Directors. [These are the associated set of
> activities.]

There is no list of associated activities that could comprehen-
sively describe every activity of this Chief Operating Executive. And
when we negotiate as part of our jobs—whether as an executive,
plumber, or teacher—the corresponding activities are not always
spelled out. There is usually no specific policy about how employees
should negotiate with their colleagues, boss, or counterparts at another company. This provides you with an opportunity.

Expand your role to include meaningful activities. No matter
your job label, you have a choice about how to define many of the ac-

tivities in your role. You can decide the extent to which you want to talk or to listen, to argue or to work together, and to treat others with disrespect or with courtesy. You are free to explore interests with the other side, to brainstorm options that meet your interests and theirs, and to ask the other person's advice or to offer advice. You can make recommendations about how to structure an agenda. In large part, the bounds of your role are set by you.

Consider the experience of two waitresses working at the same Cambridge restaurant. They discovered that each was trying to write a novel. Both saw the job of waitress as a temporary way to make a living until their first novel was accepted by a publisher.

The first waitress found her job hard work, physically exhausting, and boring. During the afternoon break between the end of lunch and the beginning of dinner, she went back to her apartment and tried to write. But the writing didn't go well, and she often found herself taking a nap instead. Each morning before work, she sat down by the computer and tried to write seriously. She found it hard to make her characters plausible and to fill their lives with realistic things to do.

The second waitress also found the restaurant work hard and physically exhausting, but not boring. She considered everyone at the table she was serving as a potential character in her novel or possibly in a later one. She kept two pads in her apron pocket, one for orders and one on which, when time permitted, she jotted notes about the people she was serving. She recorded physical characteristics of her customers, bits of conversation she had overheard, and, at other times, what she imagined the people at the table might be thinking or what they might do when they left the restaurant.

She found it much easier to breathe life into the characters in her novel by observing real people rather than sitting alone at her desk. During the long break between serving lunch and dinner, she wrote up her notes and expanded upon them. When she was writing her novel during the morning before she started work, she found herself putting to good use the people, the conversations, and the ideas that had been stimulated during the previous days and weeks. As her manuscript took shape, her reputation as an attentive and popular waitress also grew. She showed a genuine interest in those she was serving, seeing each in the role of a person with a fascinating life.

Her job was "waitress." But she expanded her job to include activities that were fulfilling to her. She gathered information about what real people looked like, how they talked, and what she imagined they thought and felt—data and ideas that she could use in her writing. She found her combined roles not only exhausting but also exhilarating.

Just as the waitress chose activities to make her role more fulfilling, you have the power to choose activities that make your role as negotiator more fulfilling. Your role can include the excitement of learning more about others, about negotiation, and about yourself.

Redefine the activities in your role. If you find that your role is not fulfilling, you may want to consider how your role is being affected by the other core concerns. A role may be unfulfilling because you feel disaffiliated from others, unappreciated for your point of view, limited in your autonomy, or demeaned in status.

Rather than passively accepting an unfulfilling role, you can shape your own role to satisfy your other core concerns. Table 9 outlines four steps you might follow. Dan recalls how applying these steps reduced unnecessary conflict between the director and associate director of a regional education program that reached millions of youth.

I received a phone call from "Paul," the director, who invited my consultation. He and "Sarah," the associate director, were in charge of the overall direction and running of the program. As their program rapidly expanded, their working relationship had corroded to such an extent that their major funder threatened to cut off *all* funding if they did not resolve their "issues."

Their conflict affected the quality of the education program. Although their offices were next to one another, they spoke only at the mandatory Friday morning meetings. Midlevel employees began to "take sides," and communication between them deteriorated. The directors spoke less frequently with employees and failed to send materials promptly. Over time, the disagreement cost thousands of wasted hours and dollars.

Through conversation with each of the directors, it became

TABLE 9

FOUR STEPS TO SHAPE YOUR CONVENTIONAL ROLE

1. Name your current role
2. List current activities within your role
3. Nominate activities to make your role more fulfilling • Add some new activities? • Modify current activities?
4. Consider deleting unfulfilling activities • No one has to do these? • Someone else should handle them?

clear that their conflict was largely a result not of differences over the direction of the program but rather over frustrated roles. Both Paul and Sarah blamed the other for "not doing what they should be doing." When I asked, "What are the other person's responsibilities?" neither had a clear answer. When I asked them what their own responsibilities were within the expanded organization, their answers were equally unclear. And now that the program had grown rapidly, neither found his or her role personally satisfying. They were overwhelmed with meaningless organizational tasks.

I facilitated a process to help them build more fulfilling roles for themselves. I met individually with Sarah, then with Paul, and walked them through the process described in Table 9. Here is how the meeting with Sarah went:

Name your current role. I took out a sheet of paper and put it in front of Sarah. I asked her to write her current job title. She wrote, "Associate Director of the Education Initiative."

List current activities within your role. Underneath her job title, she listed her current responsibilities, such as "providing input into the overall program direction," "communicating with at least three of the project coordinators," and "developing curricula."

Nominate activities to add, modify, or delete to make your role more fulfilling. I listed the core concerns, briefly described the importance of each, and suggested that we nominate some activities to make her role better meet her core concerns. Within minutes, a number of good ideas were on the table. She could organize three trainings for midlevel employees, which would address her desire for status while also enhancing the program. She could keep in contact with a variety of midlevel employees, which would enhance her affiliation with them while also enhancing their communication with her. And she could have a social dinner with Paul every other week (to express appreciation of each other's experience and to build affiliation).

None of these activities required a great deal of additional energy, and none impinged upon the autonomy of Paul. In fact, they furthered the mission of the program.

After running through these same steps with Paul, the next stage in building a fulfilling role was up to them. Paul and Sarah sat down together to discuss their suggested activities. They made clear at the beginning that all ideas were suggestions, not commitments. The discussion went smoothly because there were already a lot of ideas on the table. Within an hour, the two agreed to revised roles. They also agreed to revisit this issue in two weeks to discuss what was working well and how they might further refine their roles.

Did this process work? Paul said, "This entire process took five hours. Our mishandled conflict cost the organization hundreds of hours. The biggest regret I have is that we failed to have this simple conversation one year ago, as our project was just getting off the ground."

This same process can be used in a variety of situations to help you and others build more fulfilling roles. If you find yourself disagreeing often with a colleague, boss, or subordinate, consider initiating a discussion to clarify roles and associated activities.

When you encounter friction with another negotiator, you might run through this process from *the other person's perspective* to learn ways you can help them make their role more fulfilling. List what you think are their expected activities. What are they not doing that they could, perhaps, be doing? What are some additional activities they might do to make their role more fulfilling? Talk with them about your ideas. Treat your ideas as suggestions, not as a criticism or demand.

Appreciate the Conventional Roles That Others Want to Play

A fulfilling role can occupy an important place in our lives. Our identity becomes closely associated to the role and all that it brings—the status, the power, the affiliation. Losing that role can feel like someone is cutting off a part of us. We may go to great lengths to resist being hurt.

Consider the experience of "John Moore," a businessman who ran a chain of radio stations. He was interested in buying another station. He had to negotiate with the station's two owners: an investor and the manager. The investor owned a two-thirds share of the station and had agreed to sell it at what John considered a reasonable price. But the manager was asking as much for the one-third of the station that he owned as the investor wanted for his two-thirds.

Roger learned these facts at lunch with John when he had asked his friend if he had any current negotiation problem on which Roger's thinking might be helpful.

ROGER: Why does the manager want the money?

JOHN: Don't know. He is just greedy. Do you have a solution for greed?

ROGER: Is he married? Does he have children?

JOHN: What's that got to do with it? Yes, he is married. There's a photograph in his office of his wife and two boys—about seventh and eighth grade—in football uniforms.

ROGER: What does his wife do?

JOHN: How should I know? Well, I do know. She's on the

school board. Once, when I was there at the station, she phoned. She had a school board meeting, and he had to go home and feed the kids.

ROGER: Are there other radio stations in town?

JOHN: No.

ROGER: And how involved has he been in this station?

JOHN: He's built it up, practically from nothing, to be the best in the market.

ROGER: Maybe they don't want to move. With his wife on the school board and the kids in school, I would guess they don't want to move. On top of moving, he himself may not want to start looking for a new radio station to buy, and for a new investor to help him buy it. Why do you have to buy out the manager?

JOHN: The FCC says that in order to merge the books and offset gains of some subsidiaries against the losses of others, I have to own at least three-quarters of each station. So buying two-thirds from the investor would not be enough.

ROGER: Why don't you explain that to the manager? Offer him a fair price for that sliver between the one-third he now owns and the one-quarter he can keep. Offer him a contract to stay on as manager for a couple of years.

JOHN: It will never work. He is just too greedy.

ROGER: You know him. I don't. Maybe you're right. But you might want to try him out on the idea of getting a bit of cash now, and staying on as manager with a one-quarter interest.

About ten days later, John called up Roger. "You'll never guess what happened. He *fell* for it."

In this situation, Roger thought not only about the financial issues at stake but also about the personal issues facing the manager. He asked questions to try to appreciate how the situation looked to the manager. He recognized that the manager was probably concerned not just with money but also with fulfilling roles for himself. By selling the station, many of the manager's roles might become unfulfilling. Would he still be a *good husband?* (His wife might resent a decision to move from a community in which she is actively involved.) A *good parent?* (The children might be angry and fearful at the prospect of attending a new school and having to make new friends.) A *good manager?* (He had managed the radio station for many years, probably saw that role as a part of his identity, and found meaning it.) A *good entrepreneur?* (He may have felt mixed emotions about finding a new station to buy and a new investor to help him buy it. His current radio station was successful, but what if new ventures should fail?)

What seemed like greed to John was, to the manager, a desire for a fulfilling role as good husband, good parent, good manager, and good entrepreneur. Once the manager was offered a package that fully took into account his future role, he, not surprisingly, "fell for it."

YOU HAVE THE POWER TO CHOOSE
YOUR TEMPORARY ROLES

Jake LaMotta, a famous boxer, liked to play the role of victim in the ring. His opponents would throw punch after punch, and Jake would withdraw passively like a possum. As the opponents increased their confidence with each successive strike, they relaxed their guard. That's when Jake would unleash his attack.

Playing the role of victim was a basic strategy for Jake. His opponents almost automatically took on the opposite role of perpetrator, but not of their own volition. They reacted to the role Jake was playing. The more he played the role of helpless victim, the more confirmed they were of their strength, and Jake exploited that tendency.

As we negotiate, we sometimes fall for the same trap. We play a role in response to a role set by another person. If the other acts adversarial, so do we. If they make demands, we make demands. If they call us weak, we show our strength.

By letting others choose our role, our core concern for a fulfilling role may go unmet. We feel trivialized. And like Jake LaMotta's opponents, we put ourselves at risk of being misled.

Become Aware of Temporary Roles
You Automatically Play

Temporary roles change based upon how you are acting in the moment. In a negotiation, you have the freedom to play such temporary roles as listener, arguer, or problem solver. By giving a name to these patterns of behavior, you can become more alert to them, talk about them, and decide which ones to play.

You may find yourself habitually playing one temporary role. With colleagues, you may be the listener that everyone seeks when they have personal problems. When negotiating with colleagues who are your senior in age or social status, you may act as an accommodator. With a romantic partner, you may often play the role of problem solver.

People often pay too little attention to temporary roles. Yet these are the easiest roles you can choose to play. No one needs to assign them. You can choose to play them on your own. In the course of a one-minute conversation, a manager may play the temporary role of problem solver, listener, advisor, and advocate. Meanwhile, the conventional role of manager remains the same. Table 10 provides you with some sense of the types of temporary roles you might play as you negotiate.

Adopt a Temporary Role That Fosters Collaboration

As you negotiate, select a temporary role that feels true to yourself and that fosters collaboration. Would it be beneficial to play the role of friend? Protector? Mentor? Joker?

Consider the situation of "Jim" and "Nancy," a married couple. Nancy comes home after a long day of work. At a staff meeting, her boss blamed her for mishandling an important corporate client. When Jim comes home, she begins describing her day to him. Within one minute, he disrupts her to offer ideas on how to improve her situation.

Nancy wants to scream at him, "Why won't you just listen to

TABLE 10

COMMON TEMPORARY ROLES

Talker	Victim
Listener	Aggressor
Devil's advocate	Problem solver
Collaborator	Colleague
Competitor	Informal mediator
Accommodator	Facilitator
Compromiser	Host
"Joker"	Guest
Learner	Evaluator
Brainstormer	Option generator
Advocate	Advisor

me!" She restrains, but interrupts him and continues talking about how frustrated she feels. He now becomes offended and says, "What's *your* problem? I'm just trying to help." She feels stuck. She knows Jim's intentions aren't bad, but she feels unsupported. She walks out of the room.

In this situation, Nancy and Jim have a different expectation about the temporary role Jim should play. Nancy wants him to play the role of listener, whereas he automatically falls into the role of problem solver. While no role is inherently "wrong," some are generally more fulfilling than others.

As Nancy becomes aware of their conflicting expectations, she might suggest that Jim play a more helpful role. In a supportive tone, she might say, "I appreciate your wanting to make sure that I'm okay at work. Right now, I think I really need you as a listener. Would you be willing to do that for a few minutes, and then I'd love to get your advice on how to deal with this situation?"

Or Jim might note that Nancy is getting upset and realize that his role as problem solver does not suit Nancy's needs right now. He adopts the role of listener. It matches his desire to support her. To change roles, he demonstrates to Nancy and himself that he is now a listener: "Tell me more about your day. It sounds frustrating." She talks. He listens. Within a minute, the emotional tone of their conversation lightens. They now can support one another rather than needlessly fight.

As with Jim and Nancy, you might find it helpful to consider temporary roles that you habitually play at work and at home. Are they helpful? It takes years of education to legitimately assume the role of surgeon or lawyer, but you can adopt helpful temporary roles starting right now.

Appreciate the Temporary Roles That Others Play

At any given moment, we may fail to appreciate how another person views his or her temporary role. This lack of appreciation can generate frustration and confusion. Dan remembers such an instance in which views about roles were badly misaligned.

"Jane," a student of mine, arrived late for a job interview with a consulting firm. She was rarely late. Today was an exception, and she worried about how to explain her tardiness to her interviewer. Upon arriving at the firm, she was directed by a secretary to a conference room and hurried down the hallway.

She was happily surprised to discover that "Melissa," the interviewer, was a former graduate school classmate with whom she had worked on several school assignments.

Jane said with a laugh, "Melissa! It's so good to see you! Sorry I'm late. You know how crazy things can be this time of year!"

Melissa's response was distant and professional: "Let's get started."

Jane was startled by the coldness of the response. Was Melissa upset at her tardiness? What should she say now? Should she apologize again? Would that make her seem obsequious and unassertive? Thoughts barraged her mind, and for the remainder of the interview she struggled to concentrate.

Jane was not surprised when, two days later, she received an e-mail message from Melissa turning her down for the job.

Jane's fatal faux pas was in treating Melissa as a friend and fellow classmate, while Melissa expected to be treated as an impartial evaluator. Each acted on a differing assumption about Melissa's role. In fact, a few weeks after her interview, Jane learned from a friend at the consulting firm that her initial comments were looked upon as an informality to which she was not entitled. That perceived disrespect cost her a job offer.

Jane would have been wise to consider how Melissa saw her own role. From Melissa's point of view, she was an interviewer, and Jane's primary role was applicant for a job, not fellow classmate or friend. To avoid appearing presumptuous, Jane might have recognized the merit in Melissa's perspective:

First, thank you for scheduling an interview. I am sorry to be late. My flight from Boston arrived more than an hour after the scheduled time, and the traffic was terrible. I am ready to start, and I will try to do as well as I can in whatever time is available now. Or, if you prefer, we could meet at another time.

Rather than having Jane assume that she would get special treatment as a friend, she could have initiated dialogue demonstrating her appreciation of Melissa's formal role, saying, "Given the circumstances, I will gladly follow your lead on how formal you want this interview to be." If Jane initially overstepped her role, she could have apologized and then recognized Melissa's formal role.

The moral of this story is to appreciate how the other person sees his or her role. This is especially important if you share multiple roles with someone. Otherwise, you may surprise the other by saying or doing something that fails to meet his or her expectations.

Suggest a Temporary Role for Them

Formal roles can handicap our ability to speak openly. By suggesting that we interact on an "informal basis," we can expand our freedom to share ideas and change the level of trust between us. This is a lesson learned in an important set of negotiations forged by Lord Caradon, the British Ambassador to the United Nations.

In 1967, Lord Caradon was working to persuade the fifteen

member countries of the Security Council to support UN Resolution 242. This resolution offered a framework to settle many of the big issues in the Israeli-Palestinian conflict. He calculated that if the vote were to be taken immediately, many of the Security Council members would approve the resolution. But in order for the resolution to have the best practical chance of being implemented, he needed a yes from one of the main nonsupporters: the Soviet Union.

Soon before the vote on Resolution 242, the Soviet Deputy Foreign Minister Kuznetsov met in a private room with Lord Caradon. He requested that Caradon postpone the vote on the British resolution for two days. Caradon hesitated, fearing that the Soviet Union might use that time to its advantage to revive a competing resolution.

But then Kuznetsov surprised Lord Caradon. He made it clear that the request was not coming from his government, but from himself personally: "I am not sure that you fully understood what I was saying to you. I am personally asking you for two days."

This unusual request changed the decision facing Lord Caradon. He knew Kuznetsov, respected him, and trusted that he would do nothing that would hurt their relationship. He also realized that Kuznetsov might personally like more time to try to persuade the Soviet government to change their opinion. Caradon simply said, "Thank you. The two days are yours." He walked back to the Council chamber and announced a two-day postponement on the vote.

Two days later, the Resolution came up for a vote. The first hand raised in support of Resolution 242 was that of Deputy Foreign Minister Kuznetzov of the Soviet Union. Applause broke out in the crowded gallery of the UN chamber as the resolution was unanimously adopted.

Kuznetsov's personal request to Lord Caradon established a more fulfilling role for each of them. Kuznetsov recognized that in the circumstances then existing, it could be difficult for a British Ambassador, on behalf of the British government, to speak candidly to an official representative of the Soviet government—a government that was opposed to Resolution 242. By shifting their roles from "advocates" of their own country to informal, trusted "colleagues," it became easier to talk freely and to work side by side.

The shift to informal roles also allowed the two men to benefit from their personal trust for one another. By taking on the role of friend and colleague, Kuznetsov implied that he would use the additional time not to damage Lord Caradon or the prospects of Resolution 242, but rather to attempt to persuade his own government. Lord Caradon's acceptance of the personal request indicated his faith in Kuznetsov's intentions. The actions these two diplomats took in their informal capacity facilitated the successful vote on the UN resolution.

A CAVEAT: ROLES ARE NOT JUST "THEIR PROBLEM"

The big message of this chapter is that you have great freedom to shape a fulfilling role for yourself and others. Yet most of us do not use that freedom to the extent we could. Sometimes, we simply fail to take the initiative to expand our role. At other times, anger may jumble our thinking and cause us to play a role that serves little purpose for us or others.

Roger remembers such a time when a co-pilot's own anger jumbled his ability to act effectively in his role. Roger was a second lieutenant meteorologist in the U.S. Army Air Corps flying as a weather reconnaissance observer from Goose Bay, Labrador, to Meeks Field, Iceland. One winter day, their four engine B-17 plane, with plenty of gas aboard, was flying at about 10,000 feet. The weather was remarkably clear without a cloud in the sky, and the pilot was bored:

> To provide the crew with a little excitement, he quietly cut off the number one engine (the far left) and feathered the propeller. While the B-17 could easily fly on three engines, we were in the middle of the Atlantic Ocean. The nearest airfield, in Greenland, was closed with low clouds, and Iceland was hours away.
>
> The fear among the crew on seeing one dead engine was so satisfying to our hotshot pilot that, just for a lark, he cut off and feathered the other three engines. There was total silence in the plane as it started to glide toward the icy North Atlantic.
>
> Having scared the wits out of the crew, the pilot turned on

some switches and pressed buttons to unfeather the propellers and start the engines. Nothing happened. Only then did the pilot and co-pilot remember that to unfeather the propellers and start an engine, the plane had to have electric power. And it now had none. The whole plane was dead. Even at an airport on the ground, external power is required to start a plane's engines.

On our long glide toward the ice-cold ocean, we heard the copilot tell the pilot, "Boy oh boy. Have *you* got a problem!"

Here, we see that the co-pilot likely felt conflicting roles (and a lot of frustration). As co-pilot, he had a responsibility to ensure the safety of the plane and passengers. As victim of a practical joke, he knew the pilot had created the problem and assumed it was the pilot's job to fix it. As human being, he had an interest in survival. In anger, he reacted automatically and played the role of victim. If it were not for a young sergeant on board who expanded his own role, Roger might not have lived to tell the story:

We had on board a flight engineer, a sergeant who was to do some work on the plane when we got to Iceland. Fortunately, he remembered that we had a "putt-putt generator" on board that we could use to start the engines if we ever had to land on an emergency airstrip in Northern Greenland where there was no airbase or ground power.

Nothing made it the sergeant's job to do anything on the plane when it was flying. But he remembered the generator. Ran back. Found it. Wrapped a rope around the flywheel and pulled it several times. Fiddled with the carburetor. Wrapped the rope again and pulled it hard, this time starting the putt-putt generator. He connected the wires to the plane's system, and we had power. We had fallen only about a mile toward the ocean when the pilot got one engine going, and then all four.

We arrived in Iceland alive, relieved, and shaking our heads in disbelief at the pilot's conduct.

Unlike the co-pilot, who clearly thought it was the pilot's job to solve the problem, the flight engineer took the initiative and got electric power to the pilot, who could then restart the engines. Nowhere was it written in the flight engineer's conventional role that he was supposed to work on the plane while it was in the air. But he did.

REVISITING THE PERFORMANCE REVIEW

In this final section of the chapter, we revisit Ryan, the employee who consulted Dan about his upcoming performance review. What follows is a rough version of Dan's advice to Ryan. Because the core concern for a fulfilling role often intertwines with the other core concerns, we discuss advice to deal with each of the five concerns:

Role

Let's start by thinking about advice to improve Ryan's conventional role and his temporary roles.

Conventional role. He takes his conventional role in the organization as a given. He passively accepts the expectations of his current job such as to write memos, to work with clients, and to stay late to finish projects. He enjoys many parts of his job, but it is not as fulfilling as he would like it to be. He wants to gain leadership experience within the organization. He wants to spend more time with his family. And he also enjoys sports, but finds little time to play them because of his many commitments.

Rather than passively accepting his conventional role, Ryan might try to incorporate new activities into it. He could discuss with his boss ways to improve his role to make it more meaningful for him and for the organization. He might say, "One of my long-term goals is to be a high-level manager in this organization. Do you have any advice on activities I might try this year to gain this kind of managerial experience? Maybe there are some tasks that I could help you with?"

As for his desire to spend time with his family, he might say,

"My spouse gets home from work early on Tuesdays to take care of the kids. Could I stay later than usual on Tuesdays so I can spend more time with my kids on Wednesdays?" And with regard to his desire to pursue sports, he might discuss with his boss ways to schedule a couple of "working hours" each week coaching after-school sports at the local community center. His organization could benefit from good public relations and a more motivated employee; he gets a more fulfilling role for himself.

Temporary roles. Before he steps into the meeting, he could recognize his tendency to play the temporary role of victim awaiting punishment from his boss. In the past, he paid little attention to the areas in which his boss praised him. Rather, he waited for his boss to criticize his performance, and then he came to life and defended his actions. These roles of victim and defender did not fulfill him; nor did they foster collaboration.

Ryan might review the list of temporary roles that he could play in the meeting. Which might he adopt to advance the discussion? He might decide to play the role of listener, allowing his boss to express observations without interruption. Then Ryan could play the role of brainstormer, working with his boss to nominate ideas that could improve his performance and address his concerns.

Appreciation

As Ryan walked into the room, he tried to assess whether his boss was in a good or bad mood. He let the current mood of his boss dictate the tone of the meeting. A better approach for establishing rapport could be to set a tone conducive to appreciation. It's a lot harder for his boss to criticize him when he is sincerely praising his boss's hard work.

Appreciation has to be authentic and sincere. If Ryan flatters his boss with flowery praise, his boss may see that as manipulative behavior and take offense. Before the evaluation meeting, Ryan might prepare a list of two or three ways in which he honestly appreciates his boss and the organization. He could start the meeting by sharing one of the items on the list: "Did you know that a major reason that

I've stayed with this organization for the past six years has been because of the tone that you and the other managers have set? It is direct and efficient. It has allowed me to learn how to express my interests more clearly and have the opportunity to hone my skills."

By the same token, Ryan cannot bargain for sincere appreciation from his boss: "I'll give you two sentences of understanding if you'll give me four words of praise." Nor can he force his boss to appreciate him: "Give me empathy three times daily or else I'm leaving the company." If the boss expresses appreciation because it was asked for, Ryan will probably wonder whether the boss is being sincere or is just trying to please him.

While Ryan cannot force appreciation from his boss, he can model the behavior he wants. For example, he felt upset that his boss did not appreciate the effort he put into getting memos together in a timely fashion. Yet *he* failed to appreciate the time and effort his boss expended in compiling an evaluation of him. And Ryan failed to listen actively to his boss's positive appraisal of his work. Whether Ryan agreed with the appraisal or not, he could have listened and tried to understand how his boss saw things. Once the boss feels that his message is sincerely "heard," he is more likely to listen to Ryan.

After Ryan's meeting, he could have followed up with a short letter or e-mail to the boss letting him know what he learned from the meeting, how helpful his suggestions were, and how he will be trying to change his behavior accordingly. He might also have asked if his boss might be able to give more frequent feedback sessions. This might improve his job performance and his relationship with the boss since it would make the boss feel appreciated for his opinion.

Affiliation

Ryan and his boss interacted as adversaries. Ryan walked into the meeting on guard for an emotional "beating" from his boss. His psychological defenses were up, and he was ready to counter any "attack" his boss might make on him or his performance. The boss appeared equally protective as he told Ryan about the problems with his performance and refused to acknowledge Ryan's point of view. The behavior on both sides was more of a precursor to war than a learning conversation aimed at building a positive relationship.

A different approach could have been to set a collegial tone in which Ryan and his boss jointly faced the same challenge of making their organization work more effectively. Each of them has an interest in furthering the mission of the company. Rather than rejecting any negative feedback from his boss, Ryan might reframe the feedback in a way that builds affiliation between the two of them. After the boss tells Ryan that he needs better follow through with memos, Ryan might say:

> It's true that I did not complete that memo on time. I don't want to neglect the needs of our clients. I've been trying to juggle work and home life. Could we take a few minutes to brainstorm ways that I might be able to spend time with my family and get things done more effectively? One idea I had was that I could make a routine of checking my office voice mail when I get home from work. If anything urgent comes up, I'll be able to take care of it promptly. I can talk to my spouse about how to make sure that we have coverage for the kids when something here takes precedence. Do you have other ideas?

If Ryan did a little homework, he could discover whether or not his boss has children. If his boss is a widower with three children, he might try to establish a personal connection around shared roles as parents and organizational employees. He might ask, "How were you able to raise three kids *and* climb up the organizational ladder at the same time?" But he should ask the question only if he is honestly interested in learning the answer. Otherwise, he is not building authentic affiliation. Most people are very good at sensing the difference between affiliation and manipulation.

Autonomy

Ryan unduly limited his own autonomy in the meeting. Ryan regarded his boss's feedback as descriptions of "the truth." Any time that Ryan disagreed with the feedback, he experienced a gush of emotions screaming out, "That's not who I am!"

It might be better for Ryan to exercise increased autonomy in his own mind. He could see whatever the boss says as a hypothesis to reflect upon alone, with his spouse and colleagues, and perhaps at a later time with his boss. Rather than becoming defensive in the meeting, he then will be more able to listen without judgment. He can decide later, in the comfort of his office or home, whether or not *he* thinks he is forgetful, bad about follow through, or irresponsible in terms of the amount of time he dedicates to his organization.

What if Ryan disagrees with aspects of his boss's evaluation? He has the autonomy to choose his battles. There is no need to assert his autonomy around unimportant issues that do not have much of an impact on his future in the organization. (Is the memo issue *that* important?) If the boss says things that *do* have a significant impact, Ryan can ask questions to learn more. Then he can explain his perspective to the boss.

Because the boss submits his evaluation to the organization, Ryan apparently thinks he does not have any autonomy in the meeting. Not true. He has the autonomy to recommend ideas and information about his performance. In advance of the meeting, Ryan might prepare a memo describing what he believes to be the areas of his effective performance *and* areas in need of improvement. He could give this memo to his boss before their meeting. This memo might relieve the boss of some of the stress associated with having a great deal of autonomy in how to evaluate him. Ryan also has the freedom to prepare some questions about how he might improve his job performance or the strategic directions of the organization.

Status

Ryan seems to have fallen into the trap of assuming that status is a zero-sum concept: the more status the boss has, the less Ryan has. The meeting turns into a power game, with each trying to "one-up" the other as to whose evaluation of Ryan is "right." This is an emotionally dangerous path to go down.

Rather, Ryan can use status to stimulate positive emotions in himself and the boss. Each holds areas of particular status worthy of the other's deference. The boss outranks Ryan in terms of decision-making authority and managerial experience. Ryan outranks the boss in terms of ground-level understandings of what goes on in their organization. Therefore, Ryan wants to respect the boss in his areas of high status; and he wants to inform the boss of his own areas of high status that could help the organization.

Ryan might say, "I have had a lot of experience this year at the ground level of this organization. You have a tremendous amount of management experience. Is there any way I might brainstorm with you some possible ways to improve office morale and get junior colleagues more motivated?"

SUMMARY

In a negotiation, you always have a job to do. In most cases, however, *how* you do that job is up to you. You are free to expand the activities within your conventional role. In almost any role, you can focus your attention on aspects that are boring, dull, frustrating, and time consuming. You can define your role narrowly, limiting it to those things that you are obliged to do or that someone else expects you to do. Yet you have the freedom to shape activities in your role. Time and again, you also are free to choose temporary roles that empower you and foster joint work.

Reshaping your role can take effort. But don't give up. Give it a try. And try again. Over time, you can modify your role to your liking.

III

Some Additional Advice

CHAPTER 8

On Strong Negative Emotions

They Happen. Be Ready.

> *When angry, count to ten before you speak; if very angry, a hundred.*
> THOMAS JEFFERSON

> *When angry, count to ten before you speak; if very angry, swear.*
> MARK TWAIN

To deal with emotions, our general advice is to take constructive action. Rather than worry about labeling emotions, diagnosing their causes, and figuring out what to do, you can often overwhelm whatever negative emotions a person might have with positive ones. This is done if you express appreciation, build affiliation, respect autonomy, acknowledge status, and choose fulfilling roles.

Sometimes, however, strong negative emotions—anger, fear, or frustration—may drive the behavior of others. They may stop listening to you, stop talking, or storm out of the room. Equally true, strong emotions may affect your behavior. You may find yourself angry and mulling over something that the other person said or did. If these emotions are unaddressed, there is a strong likelihood that they will escalate and prevent a wise agreement.

For better or worse, strong emotions are not hard to find. You *do* have to pay attention to them before they overwhelm your ability to negotiate.

A CASE IN POINT

"Burger Brothers," a nationwide food chain, was negotiating with the owners of the "Super Sox," a popular sports team. Almost two years before, "Sandra," a lawyer and co-owner of the sports team, and "Bill," a lawyer for the food chain, had negotiated a commercial agreement between the two corporations that included the following provision:

> Burger Brothers agreed to pay the Super Sox $20 million dollars for the right to use the team's logo on their cups and paper bags for two years and to have the exclusive right to sell Burger Brothers fast-food products during all baseball games at the park. Further, the Super Sox agreed to market Burger Brothers and their products throughout their network—in their game books, on arena walls, in announcements at games, and the like.

Nearly two years after the initial agreement was signed, senior executives of Burger Brothers became increasingly disappointed by the limited marketing effort by Super Sox on their behalf. Problems culminated when the CEO of Burger Brothers attended a ball game and saw no advertisements for Burger Brothers anywhere save for a one-inch advertisement on the back of the game book.

Two weeks before the agreement was to expire, executives for the Super Sox initiated a meeting with Burger Brothers to renew and renegotiate their contract. Sandra arranged to meet with Bill. These two had built a good working relationship while negotiating the prior agreement, but had not communicated in person since its completion two years back.

"Hi, Bill. Great to see you," says Sandra.

"It's been a while," says Bill.

"Let's get right down to business," Sandra says with a smile. "We've enjoyed working with you and with Burger Brothers. And we would love to keep doing what we are doing. We'd even be willing to add some services—for the right price, of course."

"Forget that," Bill says, crossing his arms. "You didn't fulfill what you promised to do last time."

"What?" asks Sandra, shocked.

"You said we were going to be your base client. But I felt like we were one of thirty customers. We didn't get the services we paid for. If we decide to go forward, it's only going to be if you drop your price by at least $4 million. That's an order from Burger Brothers' CEO."

"That's not going to happen! This is the first I've heard that anything's been wrong. I worked my team hard to get things done for you."

"That's not what I hear!"

"Says who? And you can't blame me. Not now! Why didn't you raise this issue last year? Or two years ago?"

"But I didn't know the extent of things then."

"And you couldn't call me? To raise this issue now—this is absurd!"

"Absurd? Two years ago, I went to bat for you with our CEO. I got Burger Brothers to agree to the deal. If I hadn't vouched for you, none of this would have happened. And then you didn't live up to your end of the bargain. So don't tell me this is absurd!"

As the argument between Bill and Sandra escalates, their strong emotions begin to overwhelm their ability to think clearly. Despite the potential benefits of working together, they may say or do things that insult one another and jeopardize the likelihood of a renewed agreement.

This type of situation—where one person or company does not live up to the expectations of another—happens all the time and provokes strong emotions. It may be that your longtime housekeeper cleans less thoroughly than she used to but requests a raise and a two-week paid vacation. Or it may be that, two months ago, your supervisor promised to be your mentor as you move into your new role—but she has yet to find time to meet with you.

Countless other situations also provoke strong negative emotions. A person may betray your friendship, suggest that you are incompetent, or go behind your back to get a decision approved. He or she may disregard the importance of an issue to you, treat you unfairly, or ignore your ideas. The possible ways to offend someone are endless, but one point is certain: Strong negative emotions happen, so you had better be ready.

In this chapter, we offer prescriptive advice on how to deal with strong negative emotions—yours and those of others. We describe why strong negative emotions tend to make it difficult to reach agreement, and we offer a strategy to help you deal constructively with them.

STRONG NEGATIVE EMOTIONS
CAN SIDETRACK A NEGOTIATION

Strong negative emotions pose two main problems for negotiators. First, they can cause you to experience *tunnel vision,* in which the focus of your attention narrows and all you are aware of are your strong emotions. As a result, your ability to think clearly and creatively gets sidetracked.

Imagine two teams negotiating. Out of all of the negotiators, only one is a woman. Every time she speaks, the other team's lead negotiator speaks over her or looks the other way, as though she is not important enough for him to listen to. She gets angrier and angrier and becomes preoccupied with a single behavior—the other leader's lack of acknowledgment. Tunnel vision hinders her ability both to think clearly about the substantive issues and to contribute ideas—losses both for her and for the other negotiators.

Second, strong emotions make you vulnerable to the point that your emotions take control of your behavior. As your emotions escalate, you risk acting in ways that you will regret. You are likely to fail to think about the consequences of your behavior, especially the long-term consequences. In a fit of rage, for example, you may insult your spouse (and end up sleeping on the couch) or storm out of a meeting (and end up disappointing both your boss and your hopes for a promotion).

To make matters worse, emotions feed off one another. Your anger can stimulate the other person's anger, just as their anger can easily be "caught" by you. Strong negative emotions are like a snowball rolling down a hill. They get bigger as they roll along. The sooner you deal with strong negative emotions—yours and theirs—the easier it will be to stop them from running you over.

CHECK THE CURRENT EMOTIONAL TEMPERATURE

Whatever the source of strong emotions, you need first to become aware of them to avoid their escalation. One way to become aware is to check your "emotional temperature" often enough during a negotiation to catch your emotions before they overwhelm your ability to act wisely.

Take Your Own Emotional Temperature

Unlike taking your body temperature, there is no need to decide definitively whether your emotional temperature is 98.6 degrees or 100.2 degrees Fahrenheit. You do not even need to know which specific emotions you are experiencing—or even why. All you need to know is the general extent to which your emotions are starting to affect you. To take your emotional temperature, simply ask yourself, are my emotions:

Out of control? Past the boiling point. (I am already saying things better left unsaid.)

Risky? Simmering. Too hot to be safe for long.

Manageable? Under control. I am both aware of them and able to keep them in check.

To answer the question, quickly assess how manageable your emotions feel at the moment. Do you feel in control, or are you biting your tongue to stop yourself from berating the other negotiator? If you are finding it hard to concentrate on anything other than your emotions, your emotional temperature is at least "risky."

Assess Their Emotional Temperature

The people you are dealing with may also experience strong emotions, some of which are negative. If you do not notice that they are simmering with anger, their emotions may boil over and lead to unpleasant—even disastrous—results.

Herein lies a problem. When negotiating, people engage in thousands of different behaviors—whether avoiding eye contact, talking loudly, or banging a fist against the table. How do you determine their emotional temperature from such a wide variety of behaviors?

Like a good detective, look for behavior that is out of the ordinary. Although you cannot be certain what emotions another may be feeling, unusual behavior can alert you to a rising emotional temperature. Has their voice gotten louder, changed pitch, or gotten quiet—too quiet? Has their face become immobile, flushed, or red? Did they show up for a meeting unexpectedly late and without a good excuse?

With a little bit of observation, you can get some sense of another's ordinary way of acting. Are they consistently friendly? Quiet? Loud? Before you negotiate substantive issues with someone for the first time, consider having an informal meeting over a meal or coffee. Such an occasion offers an opportunity not only to build a sense of rapport and affiliation, but also to get a sense of their "ordinary" ways of acting. You will have more information from which to tell when they may be getting upset.

To get a sense of another's emotional temperature, you can also step into their shoes for a moment and consider whether they have core concerns that may currently be unsatisfied. From their perspective, how do things feel? Because you arrived late at a meeting, might they feel that their autonomy was impinged? Upon discovering that you met with their competitor, might they feel disaffiliated from you and perhaps even betrayed? Ask yourself if those concerns might be significant enough to stimulate negative emotions.

HAVE AN EMERGENCY PLAN READY BEFORE NEGATIVE EMOTIONS ARISE

The worst time to craft a strategy to deal with strong negative emotions is while experiencing them. Imagine what would happen if hospital staff waited until each new patient arrived in the emergency room before considering from scratch what they should do. There would be chaos. Instead, emergency rooms have developed standard operating procedures followed by everyone from nurses to surgeons and used with every patient who comes through the door. Negotiators need their own standard operating procedure to avoid facing strong negative emotions unprepared. Such a procedure can help you avoid letting emotions take charge.

The goal of your emergency plan is not to get rid of strong emotions. Whether positive or negative, strong emotions give you information about core concerns, underlying interests, and hidden barriers to agreement. Strong emotions can also energize negotiators to work toward reaching agreement. The passion of an enthusiastic negotiator can be contagious and encourage long-term joint work, just as the impatience of a mediator who has worked for hours and hours with two disputants may pressure them to come to agreement. Either way, strong emotions serve a useful function. You do not want to ignore emotions and lose their energy and information.

Rather, you want to be able to make a conscious choice—a

smart choice—about what to do with strong emotions and how to deal with the event that caused them. A wise course of action will take into account your emotions and your reasoning. Before you can reasonably reflect on your emotions, however, you first need to calm them.

Soothe Yourself: Cool Down Your Emotional Temperature

By soothing your escalating emotions, you enhance your ability to reflect on what your emotions might be telling you and what you should do about them. Although soothing can take many different forms, the basic idea is to engage in a behavior that brings your emotional temperature back to a manageable, calmer state. You want to be in control of your emotions, not have them in control of you.

What can you do to address your risky or out-of-control emotions? In the heat of anger or in a fit of frustration, it is hard to figure out how to soothe your strong emotions. Therefore, we suggest that you choose a self-soothing behavior *now*—while you are able to reflect clearly. Try it out the next time you find your emotions escalating in a risky direction. Here are some suggestions of things you can do in the moment:

- Slowly count backward from ten.

- Breathe deeply three times, in through your nose and out through your mouth.

- Pause. Allow yourself to sit comfortably in silence for a moment. Ask yourself what is at stake for you.

- Take a "justified" break to go to the bathroom or make a phone call. During the break, relax. Think about how to move the negotiation forward.

- Visualize a relaxing place like a sandy beach, a sunlit forest, or a symphony performance.

- Change the subject, at least briefly.

- Adopt a relaxed position: Sit back, cross your ankles, let your hands rest on your lap or the table.

- Let upsetting or offensive comments fly by and hit the wall behind you.

- Call to mind a good walk-away alternative that you have prepared.

One of the best methods of soothing is to ask yourself, "How important is this issue to me?" Some negotiators, just like some married couples, are at risk of making every issue a big issue. We can get worked up about issues that are of little importance. As Aristotle pointed out, "One can become angry; that is easy. But to be angry with the right person, to the right degree, at the right time, for the right purpose—that is not easy."

Negotiators increase or decrease the emotional magnitude of an issue depending upon how they size up that issue. Each of us has the capacity to treat an issue as a small mistake or as "the issue of all issues." During the Cold War, the crew of a Soviet trawler pulled up a New Bedford fisherman's lobster pot off the shores of Massachusetts, ate the lobsters, and was seen doing so by an American plane. The U.S. government faced a choice of how to frame the issue. Should it treat the matter as an intrusion by the Soviet Union into the territorial waters of the United States, or—as it wisely chose—a dispute over one lobster pot between a New Bedford fisherman and the captain of a trawler?

Sometimes, you may not be able to soothe yourself until the meeting or session has ended. After a negotiation, during a long break, or following a disturbing telephone exchange, you might try out one of the following:

- Listen to calming music.

- Distract yourself: Watch TV for a few minutes, make a phone call to a friend, read the paper.

- Take a walk. But don't obsess over who's to blame for the anger-inducing situation. Try to appreciate the other's perspective. Think about ways to deal with the situation.

- Forgive: Let go of the grudge.

Soothe Others: Calm Their Strong Emotions

Some negotiators express strong negative emotions in an attempt to gain advantage. They hope that we will respond to their strong emotions by offering a substantive concession. We may be tempted to placate their emotions, either to avoid a confrontation or to reduce the risk that they will do something irrational, such as walking out of a negotiation altogether. We sometimes try to "buy" our children out of their anger by getting them an ice cream cone. As they get older, the strategy becomes more costly and even less wise. "If you'll just stop your whining, I'll buy you a bicycle." "You want a car? Okay, but you'd better be happy now and stop asking for things." No chance. By this time we have taught our children to use their anger or another negative emotion as a way to get what they want.

Whether dealing with a child or with another negotiator, rewarding negative emotions sets a bad precedent. To be sure, giving in can often make angry people happy—for the time being. But they have also learned that a way to satisfy their substantive interests is to express a strong negative emotion. The stronger the better.

When anger, frustration, or embarrassment in another person is genuine, soothing their emotions can cool things off and allow you to keep a negotiation moving in a positive direction. There are several ways you can soothe the strong emotions of others:

Appreciate their concerns. Perhaps the most powerful way to soothe someone's strong emotions is to appreciate their concerns. People often want you to realize that they are angry or upset—and to see the merit in their concerns. Until you appreciate their experience, the intensity of those emotions is unlikely to diminish.

As you will recall from chapter 3, there are three elements in appreciating someone. You want to *understand* the other's point of view; *find merit* in what they are thinking, feeling, or doing; and *communicate* the merit you see:

> It sounds like you are frustrated that we haven't yet come to an agreement. [*You express your understanding.*] Given how much time you've invested in this new draft, I can understand why you feel like that. [*You communicate merit you see in the other's point of view.*]

Take a break. Rather than waiting for an angry person to blow up or walk out, you might call for a break, ostensibly for yourself, and appreciate their emotions and yours:

> I've been feeling pretty upset at how things are going, and I suspect you have, too. Let's take a fifteen-minute break to think about ways we might work more cooperatively and save ourselves a lot of time and hassle?

If a break is done effectively, it can truly soothe a negative emotion. During a break, parties should be encouraged to think not about who is at fault for the current tension but about ways of moving forward.

A short break can revitalize you and others if neither of you is too tense or upset. But strong emotions can easily be rekindled. If tension is palpable and an angry scene seems imminent, a five- or ten-minute break may offer a sense of relief but is unlikely to provide adequate time for our bodies to readjust physiologically. More time may be required.

Change the players or the place. If someone's emotional temperature has already reached the boiling point, you might want to soothe them by changing the players or the place. You might say, "Let's have our two assistants work for a half hour and brainstorm ideas for going forward. Then let's get back to this." Or you might suggest a neutral location for the next meeting. In international negotiations, locations are often selected to distance the parties from the immediate emotional pulls of the media, constituents, and colleagues. In everyday negotiations, a change of scenery can shift the emotional atmosphere. A business meeting adjourned to a coffee shop, a patio, or a restaurant can have a calming effect on the participants.

DIAGNOSE POSSIBLE TRIGGERS OF STRONG EMOTIONS

Once we calm ourselves, we need to decide what to do about the emotions that we experienced. Strong emotions are likely to reignite if we do not understand what brought them about in the first place. But figuring out the cause of an emotion can be difficult. Strong negative emotions let us know that *some* concern is unaddressed, but they do not direct us to a *specific* concern. Emotions tend to linger until we understand the message that they are conveying. It is only when we understand such information—and how it relates to the current situation—that we can take corrective action.

Consider Core Concerns as Possible Triggers

There are many possible causes for our strong emotion. We may feel frustrated by the lack of good options on the table, by hunger or lack of sleep, or by the insurmountable gap in how much money we have to spend on merchandise as compared to how much the seller is willing to accept.

Beyond such causes, a core concern often stimulates a strong emotion. If you observe that you or another is becoming upset, run through the five core concerns. Ask yourself, "Might the strong emotion be triggered by one of the core concerns? Which? What did people say or do to deprecate a core concern?"

Ask Questions to Check Out Your Assumptions

Even if you feel confident that you know what caused another person's strong emotions, question your assumption. You might slide your notes aside for a moment, look up at the person, and ask: "Is there something I said or did that upset you?"

It is all too easy to assume that we know why a person feels the way they do—when in fact we are very mistaken. One of the clearest examples of a mistaken assumption is a story told to Roger by a Harvard College classmate at a reunion:

> After midnight one night, my wife woke me with a sharp pain in her right side. It was tender to the touch. She had a slight fever, and I thought it might be appendicitis. I called a surgeon I knew, woke him up, told him the situation, and asked him to meet us at the hospital.
>
> When he realized who I was, he told me not to worry. "Give your wife a couple of aspirin," he suggested, "and put her back to bed."
>
> The doctor was certain that it was not appendicitis. I told the surgeon that I was worried and asked why he was so sure that it was not appendicitis. He said that he was fully awake and understood the situation. He said that he was a doctor, I wasn't, and that we should all go back to bed.
>
> When I pressed the surgeon, it turned out that his strong confidence was based on an assumption. He recalled that he had taken out my wife's appendix five or six years ago, and said, "No woman has a second appendix."
>
> I told the doctor that was true, but that some men had a second wife. Would he please meet us at the hospital?

BEFORE YOU REACT EMOTIONALLY, FORMULATE YOUR PURPOSE

Strong emotions inform us that a concern is probably not being met, and they rattle us to try to satisfy that concern *now*. We often feel compelled to deal immediately with strong emotions—ours and those of others. We want to alleviate the gnawing feeling inside us, or we want to extinguish any negative emotions directed toward us.

Immediate action puts us at risk of acting counter to purposes that are more important. If strong emotions are getting out of control, it is likely that each of us is reacting to the other and not acting with a clear purpose in mind. Without much time for thinking, emotional temperatures rise, as do the stakes in a negotiation. What was initially a straightforward transaction over money can become a conflict over status or autonomy.

How do you decide the right strategy for expressing your emotions? Know your purpose. Once you have a clear purpose in mind, it becomes much easier to choose a beneficial strategy to deal with your emotions.

For example, if your purpose is to educate the other party about the impact on you of their insensitive behavior, you may want to have that conversation over coffee when your client is not paying for your services. If your purpose is to get strong negative emotions off your chest, you may want to talk about the situation first with your spouse or with a trusted colleague.

In a negotiation, there are four common purposes for expressing strong negative emotions:

- To get emotions off your chest

- To educate others about the impact of their behavior on you

- To influence the other

- To improve the relationship

Purpose 1: To Get Emotions off Your Chest

It can be difficult to contain a strong negative emotion. Just as a person who is madly in love wants to tell the world, a negotiator who is extremely angry wants to release the internal tension generated by the emotion. A tempting way to release anger is to vent. Venting occurs when we openly and without censor express the extent of our anger to someone, typically to the person who caused it.

Consider the situation of "John" and "Louise," who recently divorced after seven years of marriage. They have two children. Louise takes care of them during weekdays, and John is in charge of them during weekends. For several weeks in a row, John was late in returning the children to Louise's house. After the first week that John was late, Louise said nothing. "Better to keep good relations for the sake of our kids," she thought. After the second week John was late, she still kept quiet, but was biting her tongue to do so. After the third week, Louise decided that the best thing to do would be to vent her anger at John. But was that a wise decision?

Venting can make a bad situation worse. Venting often causes more harm than good. And venting to the person who angered us can be disastrous. Think about its effect on the interaction between Louise and John. As Louise gets angrier and angrier, she comes to believe that John slighted or "wronged" her. She thinks to herself, "How dare he keep the children more hours than he is allowed?" Her frustration festers until, during his third late arrival, she marches out of her house, storms up to his car, and yells: "Can't you tell time? You're late. You're always late. This is my time with the kids, not yours! It's just like you!" He defends himself and bites back at her: "If you hadn't been late in dropping them off in the first place, then maybe they'd be home on time. But you can't take away *my* time with *my* kids. It's just like you to try to control me like that."

The intensity of the back-and-forth venting escalates. For every attack one person makes, the other constructs a justification. Each person becomes increasingly persuaded that he or she is "right." And as each gets angrier, he or she sees the situation increasingly in black-and-white terms. "I am right; my ex-spouse is wrong." As a result, each person feels *increasingly entitled* to feel upset. This process easily can lead to an explosion of emotions.

Focus on understanding, not blaming. As your emotions heat up, recognize that you might feel the desire to blame someone for causing your emotions. You mutter to a colleague, "This is all your fault that we didn't get the proposal in on time!" Or you blame yourself: "How could I have been so stupid not to make sure the proposal was sent."

Either way, blaming does not help. It typically leads to a downward cycle of self-justifications, criticism, and negative emotions.

As an alternative, refocus your attention on trying to understand the "message" underlying your emotions. This may be hard to do if your emotions are heated (in which case you should first self-soothe). But if you feel capable, dig for core concerns that might have stimulated your emotions. Understanding what has upset you or others can make you feel somewhat better. At the very least, you know what is bothering you, and you can take corrective action.

Let's see what happens if Louise uses this advice. Before John arrives, she spends a few minutes understanding her strong negative feelings. She recognizes that her autonomy feels impinged on by his repeated late arrival without first consulting her. This new understanding empowers her, and she feels a release of tension. Once John arrives, she is able to clearly express her concerns. Instead of saying, "You irresponsible parent! You didn't get the kids to my house by the agreed upon deadline," she says, "I feel upset. I understood that we had agreed upon the time to drop off the kids. Was I mistaken? I came home early from a meeting to make sure I was here." After listening to him, she decides to learn more, asking, "How do you see the situation? Do you have ideas on how we might reduce the risk of upsetting each other like this?"

Still, there are moments when your emotions feel so intense that all the rational advice in the world seems useless. You just want to vent. At such times, we urge you to do so with caution.

If you vent, be careful not to further justify your anger. When you talk with someone about your strong negative emotions, recognize that you risk creating new justifications for your anger. The person with whom you are speaking may not think that your reasons for getting upset are appropriate; but you are likely to be persuaded by your reasons. The more often you justify your anger—with a colleague at work, with a friend, or with the person who upset you—the more persuaded you become. Rather than your anger being vented, it escalates.

Stay on topic. To avoid a litany of self-justifications, avoid introducing into the conversation a list of grievances from the past.

"Well, this is just like the time that you . . ." Although John and Louise were arguing about the punctuality of dropping off their children, each strayed from the topic. Louise attacked John by saying, "You're always late." John bit back by telling Louise, "It's just like you to try to control me like that." These insults and attacks transformed a contained conflict into an uncontained mess.

Our advice: Stay focused on the current situation. Establish a rule that it is off limits to raise past grievances or to insult one another. The only issues to be raised are those that directly pertain to the current situation. Establish a second rule that if the first rule is broken, each party takes a short break to think about how to move forward productively.

Vent to a third party, not to the person who triggered your emotions. Even venting to an uninvolved person, such as a close friend, can be risky. If the friend is unconditionally biased in your favor, he or she may reinforce your negative perceptions of the person who angered you. For example, John heads to the local bar after dropping off his children. He realizes the importance of staying on good terms with his ex-wife for the sake of their children, but is frustrated by his interaction with her. He meets a close friend at the bar and immediately starts venting: "That damned Louise! She's out of control. It's like she's trying to hold the kids hostage from me. Totally out of line!"

John's friend concurs, saying, "Yeah, that sounds ridiculous! She has no right to claim your kids like that!"

Consequently, John feels increasingly justified for his self-serving beliefs, making the cycle of anger between John and Louise likely to escalate even more.

To prevent venting from turning into a festival of self-justification, we recommend that you *not* vent directly to the person who upset you. Instead, communicate your emotions to a disinterested friend or colleague who can moderate your perspective and give balance to your self-justification. For example, after dropping off the kids, John might call up a close friend who John trusts to moderate his perspective. John says, "I just got into another fight with my ex. I need to blow off a little bit of steam. Do you have a few minutes for me to tell you what happened? I'd appreciate your feedback since I don't think I'm seeing clearly right now."

Vent for the other side. If you are venting to yourself or to a close colleague, you want to be careful not to talk yourself into making the situation worse. One helpful activity is to vent as though you are the other side. What would they say? How would they describe the conflict? By venting as though you are the other side, you gain a better understanding of their perspective and consequently soothe some of your strong feelings.

Write a letter to the person who triggered your anger—but don't send it. Sometimes it is impractical or unappealing to enlist the assistance of a third party to help you deal with your strong emotions. On your own, you can do things to deal with your emotions. After the negotiation or during a break, it can be helpful to write a letter or e-mail to the person you feel has injured you. In writing such a letter, describe the impact of their behavior on you. Include a section on ways to keep the negotiation moving forward. Don't send your letter, however. Don't give it to the other person—at least not before taking a day or so to reflect with a clear head on whether such a letter will further your purposes in the negotiation. You might share the letter and the experience with a trusted colleague and get their thoughts on the matter.

Purpose 2: To Educate Another
About the Impact of Their Behavior on You

A second purpose for expressing strong emotions is to let the other person know the emotional impact on you of their actions. The other negotiator may have said or done something that had a powerful impact on your emotions. He or she can come to a greater sense of appreciation of your emotional experience if you clearly communicate the impact on you of their behavior.

For example, a young medical student was assigned a middle-aged physician as her supervisor. During hospital meetings, he routinely interrogated her on her knowledge of anatomy. When she gave incorrect answers, his fixed response was a sarcastic "Study more!" She felt singled out and humiliated by his comments. But instead of assuming his intentions were malevolent and venting at him, she set up a private meeting with him and calmly educated him about the impact of his comments on her:

"I appreciate your taking the time to meet with me. What I want to say is not easy for me to express," she said. "I feel embarrassed when I answer your questions incorrectly. I study hard and am starting to feel hopelessly unable to succeed in medicine. I have been considering dropping out of school."

His eyes widened with surprise at her comments. He confided in her that each year he chose one student who demonstrated superior academic skills. He pushed that student to excel. She was his chosen student for the year.

For this student, it paid off to describe to her supervisor the impact on her of his behavior. But what should she do if he responded with hostility, looking her in the eyes and saying, "Quit school if you must. If this isn't the right place for you, then move on."

She could respond by communicating the impact of *that* statement on her: "I feel lost at this school. It's so big. And when you suggest that I move on, it doesn't give me the guidance that I need right now." The supervisor still may refuse to help her, but at least he now has a clearer understanding of the young medical student's experience and emotional needs.

Purpose 3: To Influence the Other Person

A third purpose for expressing strong emotions is to influence the behavior of a person with whom you are negotiating. By expressing the intensity of your emotion, you demonstrate the importance of your interests.

Here we would like to distinguish between two situations. In one, negotiators honestly reveal a genuine strong emotion (that they might otherwise not disclose). They reveal their sincere feelings so that another negotiator may be moved by those feelings.

A quite different situation is one in which a negotiator feigns being emotionally upset in order to exert influence deceptively on another person. Rather than disclosing strong emotions that truly affect them, a negotiator here has become an actor and is falsely and deceptively pretending to be dominated by a strong negative emotion. This is being done, however, for the same purpose and with the same intent as the first case—to influence the behavior of another negotiator.

As we consider consciously using emotions in order to influence another negotiator, the distinction between *revealing* a genuine emotion of unknown strength that currently exists and *pretending* to have a powerful and perhaps uncontrollable emotion may not be as clear cut as the previous two paragraphs suggest. Expressing a strong emotion is sometimes a strategic act intended to influence the behavior of another person. A parent's anger—clearly expressed—can get a teenager to do chores that no amount of reasoned persuasion ever could. Your strong expression of anger may persuade others to act in ways that further your interests. To influence another negotiator to make a concession, might you storm out of a meeting? Rip up your notes? Raise your voice? And whatever you do, others may try to express strong emotions deceptively in order to influence you, perhaps to influence you to raise your offer on their house.

Expressing strong emotions can also be a way to influence another's image of you. A senior lawyer may perceive a new associate as weak, passive, and incapable of handling the tougher, prestigious clients. A young associate realizing the senior lawyer's perception of him may make a point of passionately asserting his views during meetings.

The truth about the state of one's emotions is rarely crystal clear. Fuzziness about that truth encourages negotiators to bluff, to mislead, and to act deceptively. As we mentioned earlier in this book, trusting others is a matter of risk analysis. Every embezzler is someone who was trusted—mistakenly. Be careful. Do not overload trust. At the same time, negotiators fare better to the extent that they are trustworthy and trusted. When it comes to being deceptive and misleading, be aware of the costs and risks. It is often possible and usually more enjoyable to behave in ways of which you, your children, and others can be proud.

Purpose 4: To Improve the Relationship

A fourth purpose for expressing strong emotions is to preserve or build your relationship with the other. Many negotiators deal with one another again and again. As with marriage, a failure to deal with undercurrents of tension can lead to a decreased ability to work together effectively. Each negotiator sees the other through an increasingly negative lens. Emotional residue builds until neither wants to deal with the other.

There are two key tactics to improve the relationship. First, explain your intentions for acting as you have. Too often, negotiators assume the worst possible explanation of another's behavior. Clarifying your intentions can deal with that issue. For example, the other side might suspect that you wrote a first draft of an agreement to bias it in your direction. If untrue, you can simply say, "My intention for writing up the first draft of the proposal was to help us work efficiently together, since time is short. Please feel free to suggest modifications to this, since I am assuming that nothing suggested by either of us at this point is a commitment."

Second, if you have said or done something that caused the other to develop strong negative feelings, an apology can diffuse their anger. Saying "I'm sorry" is a low-cost way to alter the course of a relationship. A well-timed, sincere apology can repair a tremendous amount of damage in a relationship. Some of the key elements of an effective apology include: recognition of the emotional impact of the action on others, an expression of regret, and a commitment not to repeat the negative action. Saying, "I'm sorry that you feel hurt," is not nearly as powerful as saying, "I'm sorry for my poor behavior and for the hurt it has caused you."

ADVICE FOR BURGER BROTHERS AND THE SUPER SOX

Let's now revisit the negotiation between Bill, the negotiator for Burger Brothers, and Sandra, co-owner of the Super Sox baseball team. If Bill and Sandra were able to rewind and redo their interaction, what advice might we give each of them to deal more effectively with their strong negative emotions?

Advice for Bill, the Negotiator
for Burger Brothers

Bill is understandably in a difficult position. He needs to keep three sets of relationships in order:

> *First,* there is the relationship between Burger Brothers and the Super Sox. For these two companies to work well together, they need to feel a sense of affiliation and trust with each other.
> *Second,* there is the specific relationship between Bill and Sandra. Bill has worked well with Sandra in the past, yet he has difficult information to deliver to her.
> *Third,* there is the relationship between Bill and the CEO of Burger Brothers. Because Bill pushed the CEO of Burger Brothers to go forward with the collaboration with the Super Sox, Bill's own credibility is at stake.

Creating an emergency plan for strong emotions. Bill recognizes that he may experience strong emotions before, during, and after his meeting with Sandra. With three relationships on the line, he takes a minute to think about his emergency plan to soothe his own strong emotions. He decides that if he notices his emotions escalating, he will take three deep breaths—in through his nose and out through his mouth. If Sandra's emotional temperature gets heated, he decides that he will first try to appreciate her perspective; and if that doesn't do much good, he will suggest a short break "to figure out how we might keep things moving forward."

Diagnosing possible causes of strong emotions. Before the negotiation even begins, Bill diagnoses the core concerns Sandra is likely to feel once he raises Burger Brothers' dissatisfaction with Super Sox's advertising. He scratches down the core concerns on a piece of paper and jots down a few notes about how each might be sensitive:

Affiliation: Sandra and I have a long-term colleagueship. She might feel I'm betraying that relationship.

Autonomy: Sandra might feel aggravated that I'm telling her now about the advertising problems. There's not much she can do now to fix the past. She may even think that I'm raising the issue to get greater concessions out of her in a future contract.

Appreciation: She will probably feel that I don't understand or value her perspective on the situation. I should make a point to ask questions about what she and the Super Sox have done for us.

Status: Because she's co-owner of the Super Sox team, she might feel demeaned in status if I question her organization's effectiveness. She might feel belittled that we are considering ceasing work with the Super Sox.

Role: Sandra enjoys playing the role of brainstormer, thinking creatively about advertising and marketing. This conversation may not go in that direction, at least not right away.

Preparing his purpose for expressing strong emotions. Bill asks himself, "What is my purpose for expressing my anger at Sandra and the Super Sox team?"

Is it to vent at Sandra? No. That would risk the potential benefits of a long-term relationship. It's probably better for me to express my frustration to my wife, who can keep my emotions and self-justification in check.

Is my purpose to educate Sandra about the impact of the Super Sox's negligence on me personally and on Burger Brothers? Yes. Our future relations can benefit if Sandra understands the problems caused by the Super Sox's lack of productivity. And if Sandra learns that the Burger Brothers' CEO was angry with me, she may develop a better appreciation of my situation. I might describe the ways that the Super Sox apparently fell through on some of its commitment to advertise Burger Brothers. I might also let Sandra know, "I told my boss that you were the greatest to work with. He agreed to go through with things based upon my advocacy of you. I don't like what has happened now. It has embarrassed me personally."

Is it my purpose to influence the Super Sox? Yes. I want to express my emotions with enough intensity that it is clear to Sandra that the situation needs to be addressed. The goal here would be for the Super Sox to improve the extent of their advertising, and perhaps to deal with any organizational issues that caused the problem in the first place.

Is my purpose to improve the relationship? Yes. On both a professional and personal level, I respect Sandra. We worked well together in the past. If I am able to treat her with respect and to work with her on ways to improve our joint work, our relationship may improve. We will have dealt with serious differences in an amicable way.

Cooling his emotional temperature. Ten minutes before he meets with Sandra, Bill notices his emotional temperature rising to the risky point. His hands are sweaty, and his thoughts are not focused. He is anxious. As planned, he slowly takes three deep breaths and feels more balanced.

With this preparation, Bill is ready for the emotional roller coaster of his upcoming meeting. He knows what to do if his or Sandra's emotions skyrocket. And he knows his purpose for expressing his strong emotions. This preparation will not only aid him in the meeting but will help him feel more confident.

Advice for Sandra, Co-owner of the Super Sox

The single most important piece of advice for Sandra is to prepare. She does not know that she is about to walk into a land mine. Good preparation can protect her from getting harmed—and perhaps allow her to walk out of the negotiation better off.

As co-owner of the Super Sox, Sandra does not have much free time. But she realizes the high stakes involved in her upcoming negotiation with Bill, so she takes a half hour to prepare. She spends fifteen minutes thinking about the Seven Elements of Negotiation (see page 207) and applying them to the facts of this situation. She spends fifteen minutes preparing for emotions that may arise.

Creating an emergency plan for strong emotions. Sandra has negotiated for years. She suspects that her upcoming negotiation with Bill will be easy; but she knows how quickly strong emotions can arise—and at the most unexpected moments. Given that, she decides that if her emotional temperature gets risky, she will pause, count backward from ten, and then think about how to respond to the situation. If Bill starts to get angry or upset, she plans to let any rude comments fly by her and hit the wall behind her.

Sandra does not have time to diagnose which core concerns might be sensitive for Bill. But she does jot down the five core concerns on her notepad so she can refer to them if need be.

Using the emergency plan. After a long morning meeting, Sandra heads to meet Bill. She is excited to talk with him about prospects for the future. As soon as he expresses his anger about the Super Sox's performance, she feels a wave of surprise and embarrassment. Thoughts run through her head: "I've worked days and nights to make the Burger Brothers' account a success! What is this nonsense Bill is saying!"

She realizes she is starting to vent in her own head, and she wants to regain a balance between reason and emotion. Before responding to Bill, she pauses, counts backward from ten, and then thinks about how to respond. Her pause helps slow down the pace of the conversation. Bill waits anxiously to hear her reaction.

Formulating a purpose. Sandra thinks quickly. She is tempted to insult Bill for daring to question the hard work of the Super Sox. But she stops herself, recognizing that her main purpose for expressing emotions is to maintain a relationship with Bill and with Burger Brothers. She realizes that Bill may be trying to use his strong emotions to influence the Super Sox to make future concessions. She needs a low-cost way to deal with Bill's strong emotions while not making any substantive sacrifices on her end. She decides to appreciate Bill's situation. It's low cost, and she can learn a lot. She takes a deep breath, then says, "I feel surprised that we have not known about your dissatisfaction. And I want to understand your concerns as best as I can. I would appreciate it if you would describe for me some of the ways you feel that we have fallen short." As she appreciates Bill's perspective, she understands more about his motives, his fears, and his hopes. She learns that Burger Brothers still wants to cooperate. She learns that Bill still respects her. And she learns that there are still plenty of avenues for joint work.

SUMMARY

Strong emotions happen—and often when we least expect them. To deal well with them, we need to be prepared. Preparation involves:

- taking our emotional temperature

- having an emergency plan:
  —to soothe strong negative emotions,
  —to diagnose the triggers of our emotions, and
  —to act with a clear purpose in mind.

While many people assume that venting is a helpful way to get rid of strong negative emotions, it often leaves us and others angrier. As we create arguments demonstrating why we are right and others are wrong, we talk ourselves into a storm. Venting can be helpful, but only to the extent that there is someone to moderate self-justifications and to keep in mind each party's perspective of the situation.

CHAPTER 9

On Being Prepared

Prepare on Process, Substance,
and Emotion

One day, by chance, Roger found himself sitting next to one of his former students on a flight from New York to Boston. He couldn't resist asking the lawyer what he remembered from the negotiation workshop years back. After thinking for a couple of minutes, the former student said he had learned and still remembered three important lessons:

Prepare.
Prepare.
Prepare.

He was a wise student. Too often we fail to maximize the benefits of our thoughts and our emotions because we fail to prepare.

There are two basic reasons why even experienced negotiators are often ill prepared. First, they may have no structured way to prepare for their negotiation. They assume that preparation entails reading case files and discussing when to set the meeting and how much money to demand or offer. Getting to know a case file, however, does little to prepare a negotiator for how to establish an effective negotiation process, how to learn about each side's interests, and how to deal with each side's emotions.

Second, negotiators often have no routine for learning from their past negotiations. Old habits are hard to break. Whether dealing with a boss, a colleague, or a spouse, negotiators tend to repeat unhelpful behaviors that elicit problematic emotions in themselves and others. Some negotiators walk into a meeting feeling fearful and anxious; others arrive overly confident. Some negotiators clam up if an offer is rejected; others storm out of the room. Whatever the circumstance, negotiators often fail to learn from their interactions and to put those lessons to use. If a meeting goes poorly, a negotiator rarely assumes blame; rather, he or she justifies the failed meeting by the conduct of the other side.

With careful preparation, you can stimulate positive emotions that enhance the effectiveness of your negotiation. To those ends, this chapter offers advice on how to structure your preparation and how to learn from past negotiations.

PREPARE IN ADVANCE OF EACH NEGOTIATION

There are three areas of a negotiation on which to prepare: on process, on substance, and on emotion. Being well prepared on the substantive issues that might come up in a negotiation and on the process for dealing with them will do a great deal to reduce emotional anxiety. Emotional preparation involves thinking carefully about steps to build good rapport and taking steps immediately prior to the negotiation to calm your anxiety.

On Process, Develop a Suggested Sequence of Events

A basic part of preparation is on the structure of the negotiation process itself. Much of the anxiety that any negotiator feels comes from the fear of being called on to make an important decision and not knowing what to say. Therefore, it is a good idea to prepare a negotiation process that will make you feel at ease.

Preparing a good process for your meeting entails thinking, alone and then with the other side, about three subjects: purpose, product, and process.

- **Purpose:** What is the goal of this meeting?

- **Product:** What piece of paper would best serve that purpose?

- **Process:** What sequence of events will produce a *product* that meets our *purpose*? For example:
    1. Clarify interests of each side.
    2. Generate a range of possible options to meet those interests.
    3. Select an option to recommend.

On Substance, Gain Perspective on Seven Elements of Negotiation

The Harvard Negotiation Project has identified seven elements that form the basic anatomy of a negotiation. (See page 207 for background.) As you prepare, canvassing the seven elements will raise both issues of process—improve communication, build a good relationship, clarify interests early, generate options before making any commitments—as well as issues of substance: What are the interests of the parties? What are persuasive criteria of legitimacy, such as precedent, laws, or market value? What are some realistic commitments that each side might make? What is each side's Best Alternative To Negotiated Agreement (BATNA)? We have found that the risk of a disconcerting—and sometimes disastrous—surprise can be substantially reduced if, before a negotiation begins, each negotiator has gone through the seven elements from their own point of view *and* from the point of view of the other side.

To see how persuasive your substantive arguments sound to the other side, try a variation of the role reversal exercise (discussed in

TABLE 11

USING SEVEN ELEMENTS TO PREPARE

1. **Relationship.** How do we see the existing relationship between the negotiators? Are they adversaries or colleagues? How would we like that relationship to be? What steps might we take to build a better relationship? Sit side by side? Use the language of colleagues? How might we build rapport and stimulate a favorable response?

2. **Communication.** Are we listening? For what should we be listening? What points do we want to communicate?

3. **Interests.** What, in order of importance, are some of our interests? What do we think are their primary interests? Which of our interests could be made compatible? What interests may necessarily be in conflict?

4. **Options.** What possible points of agreement might be acceptable to both sides?

5. **Criteria of fairness.** What precedents or other standards of legitimacy might be persuasive to both sides?

6. **BATNA (Best Alternative To a Negotiated Agreement).** If we fail to reach an agreement with them, what are we really going to do? If they should walk away without reaching an agreement with us, what good walk-away alternative do they have?

7. **Commitments.** What are some good commitments from the other side that we might realistically try for? What commitments are we prepared to make if necessary in order to reach agreement? Try drafting some potential commitments for each side.

chapter 3). Enlist a colleague to play the role of someone on the "other side" of your negotiation. You explain your side of the negotiation. Your colleague listens and takes notes. Then, you both switch roles. Your colleague plays you, the negotiator. You play the person on the other side. Your colleague repeats what you had said to him or her moments before. You, in turn, take on the role of being the person from the other side so that you hear your own words coming back at you. Note how it feels to be in another person's shoes at that moment and what their likely response might be. Then, compare observations with your colleague to gain insight into how the other side may perceive your argument. It is often highly illuminating and gives you a chance to rework your argument with the benefit of hindsight—before a negotiation even begins.

Once, when Gerhard Gesell, a federal district court judge, was a practicing lawyer, he told his younger associates that the firm had just been hired by the plaintiff in a big antitrust case. He asked them to take a week in the library, study the precedents, and outline the arguments that the firm could make on behalf of the plaintiff.

The following week the young lawyers came in, happy and optimistic. They told Gesell that it was a great case, that the plaintiff had strong arguments, and that they would surely win.

After he had heard a summary of the strong arguments on behalf of the plaintiff, Gesell told the younger lawyers the truth: The firm had actually been hired by the defendant. The young lawyers screamed in disbelief, protesting that the defendant had a terrible case. Gesell told them not to worry. They would soon talk themselves into believing that the defendant had a wonderful case, but he wanted them first to understand the strength of the plaintiff's case.

With that understanding, the young lawyers went to work on the defendant's side of the case. The defendant eventually won: The lawyers' arguments for the defendant had been fortified by their full understanding of the merits of the plaintiff's case.

A final substantive preparation activity is for you and those on your side to try to draft a public announcement that negotiators for the other side could make to their constituents if they were to accept your suggestions. This activity often demonstrates how unrealistic our own demands may be. It also reminds us of the importance of the other side's core concern for affiliation with their own constituents.

On Emotions, Consider Core Concerns and Physiology

An important part of preparation involves facing your own emotions and getting ready to deal with the emotions of those with whom you will be working. Emotional preparation requires you:

- to have a clear understanding of each party's concerns and how to satisfy them, and
- to feel calm and confident enough that you will be able to maintain a clear focus during the negotiation.

Use the core concerns as both a lens and a lever. As you prepare for your upcoming negotiation, take a few minutes to consider each of the core concerns. As discussed in chapter 2, you can use the core concerns both as a lens to understand what issues might be sensitive in the interaction and as a lever to improve the situation.

As a lens to understand. Consider which concerns might be sensitive for others in the upcoming negotiation. Run down the five core concerns. Jot down those that are likely to come into play. Will the fact that you work for a more prestigious company make them feel demeaned in status? Will the other's tendency to assert his or her autonomy make you feel disempowered?

As a lever to improve the situation. Think about ways that you can stimulate positive emotions using the core concerns. Might you begin the meeting by recognizing the particular status of the other negotiator as an expert in the substantive field being negotiated? Might you suggest to others a process for negotiating that ensures each party will have the autonomy to voice their interests without interruption?

The more clearly you can recall what happened to your core concerns and those of others in prior negotiations, the easier it will be for you to become emotionally prepared for an upcoming negotiation. The emotions that arise in your negotiation will be less likely to surprise you.

For most of us, however, recalling our feelings during a past negotiation is extremely difficult and highly unreliable. When we think how difficult it is for us to remember what we had for dinner last Wednesday, we realize how difficult it is to recall past experiences and how vulnerable memory is to error.

To reduce the errors of memory, jot down notes during your interaction about times when someone says or does something to appreciate or devalue the core concerns of another. After the session ends, get the perspectives of colleagues. Whose core concerns did they think were respected or trampled upon? Why? While the negotiation is still fresh in your mind, record these observations, as well as some ideas about what might be done differently in future negotiations. You can create a long-term record that can be used over time to tease out key behavior patterns of negotiators.

Before your next negotiation, pull out your notes. Read them and let yourself recall how you and others felt and what you learned. Think about how to put those lessons to use to improve the upcoming interaction.

Visualize success. Before professional skiers start down a steep slope, they often try to visualize themselves skiing beautifully down the hill, skillfully avoiding trees, rocks, and other skiers. The same approach can work for you as you visualize yourself negotiating. Picture yourself at ease, setting a positive tone, seeking to build rapport, picking up on another's cues, and moving toward a productive working relationship.

Imagine yourself at the beginning of your upcoming negotiation—right as you greet the other negotiator. How are you likely to react if the other negotiator treats you as an adversary, holding you at a distance? Are you prepared to reframe your affiliation as colleagues working together on important issues? How do you want to introduce yourself to set the right emotional tone for the meeting while acknowledging status concerns? Try out different lines to see what feels right.

"Jan! Good to see you again. How have you been?"

"Dr. Jones? I'm Professor Smith. Please call me Melissa. May I call you Tom?"

"Happy to meet you. I have heard good things about you. I am looking forward to getting your ideas about how we should go about settling this problem."

You also may want to do some preparatory work on how to enlist helpful feelings in the other party. Prepare and rehearse a few good lines that ask for their advice, demonstrate appreciation for their contribution to the negotiation, and acknowledge the other roles they play. Whatever approach you take, make sure your questions and comments reflect an honest interest without being too intrusive.

Keep your physiology in check. The core concerns will be of little help to you if your anxiety, fears, or frustrations overwhelm your ability to think clearly. Thus, take some time immediately before a negotiation to soothe pre-meeting jitters and other strong emotions.

Use relaxation techniques to calm your nerves. A few minutes of deep breathing can help you relax and focus your efforts. Another exercise that can help soothe your emotions before a negotiation is progressive muscle relaxation. This activity can last about fifteen minutes. Start by sitting in a comfortable position, perhaps in your car before the meeting. Breathe deeply. Focus on your feet. Curl your toes and feel the tension. Hold it for a second and then relax. Working your way up, tighten each of your muscles as you would clench your fist and then relax, letting the tension disappear. Concentrate on tightening and relaxing every muscle from the back of your calves to your shoulders.

When you have finished, put your chin down and roll your head slowly to the right until your ear is above your shoulder and hold for a second or two. Roll your head back and around so that the left ear is above your shoulder and hold the position for a moment. Lift your head, square your shoulders, and you should feel more relaxed and ready to go.

Prepare an emotional first aid kit. As you learned in chapter 8, strong negative emotions can overwhelm your ability to think clearly. To keep your physiological arousal in check, remind yourself of the symptoms that indicate your emotional temperature is rising. Bring to mind a single behavior or two that you plan to use to keep your cool. If you feel increasingly upset, is your plan to count to ten or suggest a short break?

Check your mood. It is important to stay aware of your mood—whether you are generally feeling positive or negative. What feelings might you bring into the room? Despite your proactive emotional preparation, a bad mood can raise your level of physiological arousal and make you more likely to lose control of your own behavior.

The trigger of a bad mood is often hard to identify. It may be caused by someone's mistreatment of you, by the fact that it is a Monday morning, or by neurochemicals that "decided" to affect you today.

Whatever the cause, becoming aware of your mood allows you to moderate its impact on your behavior in the negotiation. If you are in a negative mood, you might let others know so that they do not misattribute your mood to something they said or did. You might say to a colleague, "These Monday morning meetings always put me in a bad mood. My apologies in advance if I'm a little on edge." At the least, you can monitor your own behavior to make sure that you do not say or do things that will sidetrack the negotiation.

If you realize you are in a negative mood, decide to improve it. You often have the power to break out of your current mood rather than be a prisoner to it. Simple things like making sure to get adequate sleep and a good meal can be extremely helpful. Before walking into the negotiation, you might take a few minutes to recall pleasant memories, walk outside, or talk with a friend who can elevate your mood. During the negotiation, you can model a calm, confident mood—by sitting up in your chair, talking with confidence, and co-managing the negotiation process. After a while, you may feel more confident.

Review After Each Negotiation

Spending time in the school of hard knocks can be an excellent learning experience for every negotiator. If you pay attention, you can learn as much from failures as you can from your successes. Like other forms of on-the-job training, negotiation is greatly helped by a conscious effort to put what you are learning into practice.

Unless negotiators develop a habit of reviewing their negotiations and consciously articulating lessons that are there for the taking, most of that hard-earned knowledge fades away. The wisdom that is buried in your brain becomes unavailable unless you bring it out as a guideline for action. By reviewing a negotiation promptly after the fact, you can convert an implicit understanding of what happened into an explicit guideline for the future. You can consider how to apply that guideline in your interactions with your spouse, boss, colleagues, negotiating counterparts, and others. Although the context of your negotiations may vary, your ability to achieve your goals will consistently improve.

Set aside thirty to sixty minutes following a negotiation session for review. A partner in a Washington law firm took this advice to heart and was able to convince her partners and associates to try it out. After every negotiation, her firm's lawyers would come back to the office and meet for an hour to review. Instead of having the usual bull session about the negotiation that had just ended, they put that time to good use in an organized examination of what had taken place. The lawyers found that purposeful review was far more valuable—and even more enjoyable—than just blowing off steam.

You can review with your fellow negotiators, a colleague, or by yourself. If there were several negotiators on your side, it is a good idea to invite them all to participate. The value of their involvement stems from the fact that different participants observe and recall the same events in distinctly dissimilar ways. In a multi-participant negotiation, there are so many things happening so quickly that it is often like the fable of the blind men and the elephant. Touching different parts of the elephant, each blind man had a completely different picture of what the animal looked like. Getting the varied perspectives of several people is likely to make each a little more humble about "knowing" what happened, and each will have a better sense of the interaction.

If you have difficulty in persuading your colleagues to join you in reviewing a negotiation, do not pass up the chance to make the most of immediate hindsight. Reviewing a negotiation, even by yourself, is an invaluable opportunity to learn as you go along. On your drive home from work, for example, you might take a few minutes to review your day's negotiation.

Determine WW and DD—What Worked Well and What to Do Differently

Some people avoid reviewing the negotiation because they are afraid that they will be judged and criticized. It should be made clear that the purpose of a review is to help people learn from their experiences in the negotiation. A simple and powerful way to review a negotiation is to consider WW and DD: what Worked Well and what to Do Differently next time.

To start your review, good questions to ask are: "What did the negotiators on the other side do well? Why?" You may be able to learn something from the other negotiators by reviewing what they said or did to improve the negotiation process. Did they ask questions that got everyone talking about their interests? Did they propose an informal lunchtime meeting before your next negotiation to build affiliation?

Conversely, during the negotiation what did the other party do that was probably a mistake on their part or something that could have been done more effectively? If you were going to share honest advice, what could you suggest they might want to do differently next time? Why?

Having reviewed what worked well for the other side and what they might want to do differently, you can go through the negotiation asking the same questions about your own performance. During the negotiation, what specific things did your team do that appeared to work well?

And finally, what mistakes might you have made? Why? Can you now turn these into a few guidelines for the future? What will you want to repeat and what will you want to do differently? After creating guidelines, imagine how they might be applied in different cases, whether with family members, colleagues, or representatives of other organizations with whom you deal.

Focus on Emotions, Process, and Substance

As you review what worked well and what might have been done differently, focus on three important subjects: emotions, process, and substance. What worked well with how you and the other party managed each of these issues? What might be done differently?

Check your memory for the emotions that each of you appeared to experience. Think about what seemed to annoy you, excite you, interest you, or anger you. What kinds of things might you do next time to soothe escalating negative emotion?

The easiest emotions to recall may be the ones that arose from expressions of appreciation—or lack thereof. Run through your core concerns to consider what feelings may have been generated in you and in others:

1. *Appreciation*
   Did you feel understood, heard, and valued for your point of view?
   Did the other side feel appreciated?

2. *Affiliation*
   Were you treated as a colleague? (or as an adversary?)
   Do you think they felt treated as a colleague?

3. *Autonomy*
   Do you feel that your autonomy was impinged upon?
   Do you think they felt their autonomy was being respected?

4. *Status*
   Do you feel they respected your status in areas where it was deserved?
   Did you respect theirs?

5. *Role*
   Did you feel satisfied with the activities you performed within your role?
   Did you adopt temporary roles that felt fulfilling and useful?
   Did you broaden their role by asking for their advice or recommendations?

With regard to process, you may want to recall whether an agenda was set, how it was set, and by whom. To what extent was the agenda followed? Did it streamline or impede the progress of the negotiation? Throughout the negotiation, how did people decide what to talk about and how forthcoming they would be? What worked well, and what might be done differently in the future?

Consider how the agenda might be improved and turned into a possible standard agenda. This revised agenda could be the basis of an agenda for the next negotiation.

To review substantive success, simply consider what worked well and what to do differently regarding each of the seven elements discussed earlier in this chapter. For example, what questions did you ask that worked well in helping you discover the interests of the other side? What might you do differently next time? In the future, how might you encourage more creative brainstorming of options?

Keep a Journal of Lessons Learned

Create a journal to record what you learn from your negotiations. Write down your thoughts in a bound notebook or put them on your computer. Record what you have learned from your own successes and mistakes as well as from the skills and missteps of those with whom you have negotiated. Over time, you will have your own personal negotiation guide.

As you articulate the lessons you learn, your brain will tend to store that information and have it ready for use. The more often you recall and use those ideas, the more you will find them at your disposal.

In a class we teach on the role of emotions in negotiation, students are required to keep a weekly journal about their experiences in dealing with the core concerns. We spend two weeks exploring each of the core concerns, starting with autonomy. During the first week, students are asked to observe and document the ways that their concern with autonomy had an emotional impact on them during their daily interactions with others. Throughout the second week, the role of students becomes more active: They are asked to respect their autonomy and that of others in their day-to-day interactions. They write about what worked well and what they might do differently in the future to appreciate that core concern more effectively.

As the weeks progress, students learn to observe and appreciate core concerns, and they develop skills in learning from their negotiation experiences. At the end of the semester, we ask students to review their journal entries and to write a final paper on what they think they have learned. Reflecting upon their thoughts, feelings, and actions helps their learning stick in their heads.

SUMMARY

Preparation improves the emotional climate of a negotiation. A well-prepared negotiator walks into a meeting with emotional confidence about the substantive and process issues, as well as with clarity about how to enlist each party's positive emotions.

There are two important activities involved in effective preparation:

- *Establishing a routine structure of preparation.* You want to prepare in terms of the process of the negotiation, the substantive issues, and the emotions of each party.
- *Learning from past negotiations.* Experience is of little future value unless you learn from it. After a negotiation, review the interaction in terms of process, substance, and emotions. Ask yourself what each party did that worked well and what could be done differently in the future.

CHAPTER 10

On Using These Ideas in the "Real World"

A Personal Account by Jamil Mahuad, Former President of Ecuador

A fifty-year boundary dispute between Ecuador and Peru ended through the successful negotiation between Jamil Mahuad, president of Ecuador (1998–2000), and Alberto Fujimori, president of Peru (1990–2000).

President Mahuad has taken two negotiation courses at Harvard University—one several years ago with Roger and a seminar more recently with Roger and Dan that explicitly articulated the core concerns framework. During our seminar, President Mahuad realized the extent to which he intuitively had used the core concerns to help resolve the Peru–Ecuador border dispute. We invited him to contribute this chapter to share with readers his creative use of those concerns.

I took office as president of Ecuador on August 10, 1998, after serving six years as mayor of Quito, my country's capital.

The main motivation for entering the presidential race was to alleviate poverty and to reduce inequality in my Nevada-sized Andean country of 12 million people. My political strategy was to replicate at a national level the successful formula that I had used while mayor of Quito's 1.2 million people. My formula was: "Promise attainable projects, deliver on my promises, and stay close to the people." While I was mayor, *Fortune* magazine considered Quito one of the ten Latin American cities that greatly improved the quality of life of its citizens.

As I took office, however, the Ecuadorian economy was spiraling into—arguably—its worst economic crisis of the twentieth century. Simultaneously, political, military, and diplomatic experts foresaw an imminent and perhaps unavoidable new armed conflict with Peru.

THE PERFECT STORM

If you have read *The Perfect Storm* or have seen the movie based on the book, you'll have the right mind-set to understand Ecuador's situation in 1998 and 1999. The film depicts how, in October 1991, the unique combination of three immense meteorological events produced a storm stronger than any in recorded history. A hurricane from the Caribbean and two fronts from Canada and the Great Lakes converged and fed each other in the Atlantic. The storm trapped a small fishing boat from Gloucester, Massachusetts, and doomed its entire crew.

Here's where the analogy comes through. In 1998–1999, Ecuador was suffering from the once-in-a-century combined effects of:

- The coastal destruction left by El Niño floods (the largest in five hundred years)

- Record low-level oil prices (oil then accounted for around half of the Ecuadorian exports and the government's revenue)

- The Asian economic crisis (the first global economic crisis)

These factors came on top of a fiscal deficit of 7 percent of the GDP; the final puffings of a crashing financial system; and a physically destroyed and paralyzed private sector. The inflation rate was 48 percent and the debt to GDP ratio was more than 70 percent—both the highest in Latin America.

Consequently, international creditors—mistrusting Ecuador's capacity for servicing its debt—were demanding full repayment of loans at maturity and closing their lines of credit.

This economic meltdown demanded immediate attention. My top short-term priorities were to reduce the fiscal deficit and consequently decrease the inflation rate; to reconstruct the Pacific coastal area of the country recently devastated by the flood; and to restore the country's credit worthiness through a program with the International Monetary Fund that would get new financing for my social programs, mainly health and education.

Nevertheless, an unexpected twist in the international front forced me to change priorities and work first to avoid a war with Peru. I considered this situation to be my first and most important responsibility morally, ethically, and economically. An international war would have escalated our already critical situation into a desperate one. How could Ecuador face an international war with the economy already in shambles? I needed a definitive peace accord with Peru in order to reduce the military budget, to dedicate our scarce resources to invest in social infrastructure, and to focus our attention and energies on growth and development.

THE CURRENT SITUATION

The long, tough, disappointing history of armed conflict with Peru represented for Ecuadorians a painful wound. Ecuadorians felt abused, stripped of their legitimate territories by the force of a powerful neighbor supported by the international community.

Here was the scenario the moment I took office:

- *"The oldest armed conflict in the Western Hemisphere."* The United States State Department called the Ecuador–Peru border dispute the "oldest armed conflict in the Western Hemisphere." Its roots can be traced back at least to the discovery of the Amazon River in 1542 by the Spanish conquistador Francisco de Orellana or, even before that, to the 1532 precolonial Indian war for the control of the Inca Empire between the Quiteño Atahualpa (now Ecuador) and the Cusqueño Huascar (now Peru).

- *The largest land dispute in Latin America.* The territory historically claimed by both Ecuador and Peru was bigger than France. It constituted the largest disputed territory in Latin America and one of the largest in the world.

- *Numerous attempts to resolve the conflict had failed.* Since the early nineteenth century attempts to reach a solution consistently failed. The countries had tried war, direct conversation, and amicable intervention by third parties, mediation, and first-class arbiters including the King of Spain and President Franklin Roosevelt. None yielded a positive result.

The last period of this conflict started in 1942. After an international war between Ecuador and Peru in mid-1941 and following the Japanese attack on Pearl Harbor in December 1941, the United States pressed Ecuador and Peru to end definitively their land dispute. In 1942 in Rio de Janeiro, the two countries signed a treaty called the Protocol of Peace, Friendship and Limits. Known in short as the Rio Protocol, this treaty was guaranteed by Argentina, Brazil, Chile, and the United States.

The Rio Protocol established that part of the boundary between Ecuador and Peru would be a watershed (a ridge of high ground) between the Santiago and Zamora rivers. It turned out, however, that between these two rivers there was not a single watershed, but a third river, the Cenepa. As a result, out of a 1500 kilometer-long block of land marked frontier, approximately 78 kilometers remained an "open wound."

Armed conflict erupted in 1981 and again in 1995, but did not settle the issue. On the contrary, more bitterness and mutual mistrust developed. This zone was epitomized by the outpost of Tiwintza, a small area of land where soldiers from both countries had been killed and buried. Tiwintza became a heroic symbol to each country.

The post-1995 negotiation process had advanced important agreements regarding future joint projects, mutual security, trust, commerce, and navigational rights over some tributaries of the Amazon. Nonetheless, all this progress was contingent on a final agreement over Tiwintza.

As an almost final effort to overcome entrenched positions, Ecuador and Peru asked a special commission for a nonmandatory but morally important opinion (a *Parecer*) on the issue. The special commission was known as a Juridical–Technical International Commission and included representatives of Argentina, Brazil, and the United States. The opinion of the commission was released a few weeks before I was elected president. It expressed the view that Tiwintza was part of the sovereign territory of Peru. That opinion, contrary to the situation on the ground where Ecuadorian troops had been for decades, stirred up escalating hostility between the two countries.

By the time I took office, the troops from Ecuador and Peru had occupied the previously agreed upon demilitarized zone. They faced one another so closely that, in some places, they could shake hands and say *Buenos días* before raising their rifles. The Ecuadorian military command briefed me that a Peruvian invasion starting a few hours after my inauguration was a likely scenario. Peru would most likely provoke not a localized but a generalized armed conflict. The magnitude of this risk was perceived only by the most informed echelon of society. The rest of the country was immersed in their struggle to survive the economic difficulties and was distracted temporarily by the new president's inauguration.

THE CHALLENGE: AGAINST ALL ODDS

Upon stepping into office, pursuing peace with Peru would require:

- *Belief.* There would have to be the popular belief that the war *could* be resolved. Myths are almost impossible to debunk;

the intractability of the problem with Peru had deep roots in Ecuadorians' flesh and souls.

- *Civic participation.* Making peace between Ecuador and Peru would have to be a "people's project," not a government issue. There would need to be a boost in participation of the people represented by any legitimate organization or group.

- *Trust.* Cooperation and mutual trust would need to be elicited from all sectors in this fragmented country.

- *Political support.* A formula for peace would need to be created. It would have to be acceptable for both countries and for many different sectors in each country.

- *Economic stability.* There would need to be ways to bring economic stability to a country on the verge of war. In such a moment of distress, how could the government go about dictating badly needed, but unpopular, economic adjustments that would compromise the national unity and governability of Ecuador?

- *A clear, coherent, comprehensive action plan.* The resulting plan would need to be not only military but also economic, political, and international in scope.

PREPARING FOR PEACE

Since the purpose of this chapter is showing the core concerns in action, I'll focus my attention on the negotiation strategy of the border conflict and some interactions with my colleague, President Alberto Fujimori of Peru, while ignoring the complications of the economic situation in Ecuador.

I needed a talented governmental cabinet to carry out peace efforts. Dr. Jose Ayala, allegedly the most respected Ecuadorian diplomat, had been minister of foreign affairs and had conducted peace negotiations. I asked him to remain in his role. General Jose Gallardo had been minister of defense during the most recent armed conflict in 1995; that conflict had ended with an Ecuadorian military victory. I appointed General Gallardo to be minister of defense. In short, I appointed the chancellor of peace and the general of war as members of my cabinet. This was done to send a clear signal: Although Ecuador was openly inclined to a peaceful solution, we were ready to defend ourselves fiercely if necessary.

Chancellor Ayala informed me of the general perception that nearly every contentious issue had been agreed upon by the two diplomatic delegations. The remaining point, the territorial dispute of the zone symbolized by Tiwintza, was something that only the presidents themselves could decide. It required a final stage of diplomacy at the highest level—"Presidential Diplomacy" as the press labeled it.

I phoned Professor Roger Fisher at his Harvard Law School office and invited him to come to Quito and join the Ecuadorian government team to analyze the current situation, brainstorm possible approaches, and prepare a negotiation strategy.

When Roger arrived in Quito, we worked on various fronts simultaneously. We carefully reviewed with the ministers of defense and foreign affairs the up-to-date military and diplomatic facts. To get everybody on the same page, Roger offered, for the benefit of some cabinet and staff members connected with the negotiation, a half-day presentation of his classic Seven Elements of Negotiation and some useful techniques for their application.

Due to the current tensions, a personal meeting of the two presidents was most unlikely to occur. However, in preparation for an eventual encounter with President Fujimori, Roger and I examined ways to start a personal working relationship.

The first two or three days in any new job can be hectic. A presidential office is no exception. Our meetings were frequently interrupted by urgent events. We had some of our sessions at odd times and places. I remember slipping Roger into my office between two scheduled appointments and meeting him in the dining room of my residence in the palace after eleven at night.

KEY ELEMENTS IN BUILDING EMOTIONAL RAPPORT

In a negotiation process, the relationship among the negotiators is as important as the substance of the negotiation. My first strategic decision was to build upon the existing working relationship already established between the two national negotiation teams. My nondelegable, crucially important mission was to build personal rapport with President Fujimori, a man I had not met. It was a challenge to figure out how I would do that.

In my third day in office, I received an unexpected call from President Cardoso of Brazil. He invited me to a personal meeting with President Fujimori in Asuncion del Paraguay, where all three of us were scheduled to be thirty-six hours later for the inauguration of President Cubas.

Two facts were clear to me. I badly needed that first encounter. And I was not yet ready to tackle the substance of the problem. How could I communicate the seriousness of my intentions to President Fujimori without giving him the impression that I was just buying time and procrastinating?

Appreciation: Show Your Understanding of His Merits and Difficulties

Our team agreed to make it clear to President Fujimori that I appreciated his years of involvement in the boundary problem and the knowledge he must have derived from that experience. That assessment of President Fujimori's situation would have been plainly true for any dispassionate observer. I expected that such initial recognition would help us find an emotional common ground to serve as a basis for future conversations. My preparation with Roger started like this:

ROGER: What is the purpose of your first meeting with President Fujimori?

JAMIL: I see two purposes. I want to get to know him and his vision about the current situation. And I want to get his com-

mitment that we are going to exhaust dialogue before stepping into war. For these purposes, I would like to listen first
and ask him questions.

ROGER: Great purposes. But if you go after him with a lot of
questions, he may feel as if the FBI is interrogating him. He's
likely to clam up. An easier and perhaps wiser approach
would be to have President Fujimori come to feel that he
knows *you*. Be open. Start by laying some of your cards on
the table.

That was precisely what I did. Using stories, historical examples,
and anecdotes, I explained to President Fujimori how I understood
the difficult situation he was facing. I asked for his reciprocal understanding of the extremely complex scenario I was acting on. He responded well, although cautiously. In a soft, tranquil voice, he stated,
"My three goals when I started my presidency were to eliminate hy-
perinflation, to dismember the Shining Path guerrillas, and to finish
the border issue with Ecuador. I have accomplished the first two already. The third one must be concluded as well."

That gave me the opportunity to express frankly my admiration
for his work on both of the first two issues, which was universally ap-
plauded, while adopting a wait-and-see attitude about the third.

Affiliation: Find Some Common Ground

A major task was to change the widespread perception of the bad relationship between the two countries. This task was faced by President Fujimori and myself, as well as by our staff and officials, the
media, and the public at large. For years, each country had regarded
the other as an enemy.

President Fujimori and I agreed that a goal should be to have the
public in each country come to see that we were working together,
side by side, toward the settlement of the centuries-old boundary
conflict.

Since "one picture is worth a thousand words," Roger suggested
that I arrange for a photograph to be taken of the two presidents. I

said that would not be a problem. The media would be present before and after our meeting. Rather than a picture of us shaking hands or standing next to each other, however, Roger wanted us to be sitting, side by side, each with a pen or pencil in his hand, both looking at a map or a pad on which there might be some kind of draft proposal. We would not be looking at the camera or at each other but rather working. Such a photograph might help convince third parties, the media, and the public that things had started to change for the better. The photograph would make clear that the presidents were in a collaborative effort, tackling the boundary problem together.

When I returned from Paraguay, I showed Roger a newspaper with a front-page photograph of the two presidents working together. The photograph is reproduced on page 193.

I told Roger that I knew the photograph was intended to influence the public. What surprised me was the extent to which the photograph also influenced President Fujimori and me. Looking at the photograph, President Fujimori said that the public in each country would now be expecting us to settle the boundary. We had publicly undertaken that task, and we owed it to the people in each country to succeed.

Status: "I'll Recognize His Seniority"

President Fujimori and I met for the first time in Asuncion. We were in the presidential suite kindly offered by the Argentinean President Carlos Menem as a neutral territory. At that time, President Fujimori had been president of Peru for eight years and I had been president of Ecuador for four days.

"You can make a first impression only once," I reminded myself. "Stating the evident will not harm my position. Contrarily, it will convey the image of an open, objective person," I thought. "I'll recognize his seniority, a personal matter where there's no debate, and I will not accept his substantive proposals about delicate matters where there's a hot debate."

I said, "President Fujimori, you've been president for eight

EDICION
PRIMERA

EL UNIVE

ago de Guayaquil, Ecuador ■ AÑO 77 ■ Nº 334   EL MAYOR DIARIO NACIONAL

Associated Press

■ ASUNCION, Paraguay.— Los presidentes de Ecuador, Jamil Mahuad, y de Perú, Alberto Fujimori, dialogaron ayer en un hotel de esta capital sobre el proceso de paz, y ratificaron su voluntad de continuar las negociaciones para llegar a la firma de un acuerdo definitivo; Sin embargo, no precisaron la fecha en que las comisiones de ambos países se reunirán.

Mahuad y Fujimori ratificaron esfuerzos para la paz

Se reanudarán los diálogos

This photograph on the front page of an Ecuador newspaper helped change the political climate in 1998 by showing presidents Mahuad of Ecuador and Fujimori of Peru working together side by side.
(Courtesy of AP/Wide World Photos)

years. I've been a president for four days. You have negotiated with four of my predecessors. I would like us to benefit from your extensive experience." I asked him, "Do you have ideas on how we might deal with this border dispute in a way that would meet the interests of both Peru and Ecuador?"

I recognized his seniority with courteous gestures, which were reciprocated by him. For example, I always made sure he entered rooms first as the senior president. In this way, I acknowledged and respected his seniority, a particular status of President Fujimori. I also acknowledged my own particular status as president and as a connoisseur of the Ecuadorian reality.

To recognize areas where President Fujimori held high status did not imply that I was agreeing with him or with his position. Contrarily, when combined with showing appreciation, honoring his status gave me room to manifest my openly discrepant standings without endangering the relationship.

Autonomy: Do Not Tell Others What to Do

Autonomy is a core concern for human beings, particularly sensitive for figures like politicians who are in positions of authority. For many years, Ecuador and Peru refused to negotiate with one another, each fearing that they would be seen as "giving in" to the other's demands. No politician likes to be seen as a puppet of anybody else, especially when each one is on a different side of a centuries-old conflict.

It would be dangerous for a president to do something that would make our constituents suspicious or otherwise put us in a difficult position in our own country.

In all our meetings, I was very conscientious to respect his autonomy and to ensure my own. It would have been deadly wrong, for example, to try to *tell* President Fujimori what to do. Rather I *asked for his perceptions and reactions* on how we two presidents might best settle this protracted and costly boundary dispute.

My personal respect for him did not imply that I was agreeing with him or with his demand. "I simply cannot ask Congress and the people to give in to the demands of Peru. I'm not going to do it. Were I to do it, Congress would never agree; nor would any Ecuadorian. That's a dead-end road. What are your alternative ideas on how we might move forward toward a peaceful agreement?"

I asked President Fujimori to appreciate the fact that the Ecuadorian president, Congress, and people would never concede to this Peruvian claim. Our autonomy would be crushed.

Role: "Us" Means "Us" for Both Sides

Negotiators play multiple, simultaneous, sometimes contradictory, overlapping, or complementary roles. In an effort to settle this long-standing boundary dispute, each president would have a crucial job. Each would have the task of bringing his own constituents to accept a settlement of the boundary. I saw my role as leading two simultaneous negotiations. One role, obviously, was as negotiator with President Fujimori. The other role, not so obvious but equally important, was my role as a negotiator with the people of Ecuador, its institutions, and representative organizations.

I recognized that President Fujimori had the same two roles and faced the same tasks. Therefore, I proposed to him we not do anything to harm each other's legitimacy as authorized representatives of our peoples. For instance, it would have been self-defeating to claim that a treaty was good for Ecuador because it was bad for Peru—or vice versa.

On the contrary, I saw that the role of each president was to demonstrate that an agreement was good for both countries, good for the region, good for trade, good for economic development, and good for the alleviation of poverty. We needed a win-win proposition. In crafting that proposition, our roles were both stressful and full of personal meaning.

Too often in international affairs, the goal is seen as obtaining a commitment from the other side. The media keep asking: "Who backed down?" "Who gave in?" "Did you reach an agreement?" "No? So the negotiations failed?" They want to see us playing the role of the victorious hero defeating a deceitful enemy. But "us" means "us" for both sides. In a negotiation, the most useful and powerful outcome may be an emotional commitment to continue working together in order to implement a peace agreement after signing it. Working together did not suggest that either of us gave up our liberty, our discretion, or our autonomy.

Rather, we transformed a problem into an opportunity. That required a new conception of the roles we played: a shift from opponents to colleagues, from positional bargainers in a merely distributional zero-sum game to joint problem solvers inventing new options to increase the size of the pie and the scope of possible outcomes.

Core Concerns as a Bundle

At some moments, the situation called for intertwining different core concerns and reinforcing them at different levels. One particularly challenging circumstance stands out. The nonbinding opinion (*Parecer*) of the international experts gave a big push to Peru's claim to Tiwintza. It would have been impossible, however, for any Ecuadorian president to yield to the claim without losing legitimacy, demeaning his presidential status, betraying his role, and risking his people's appreciation and affiliation. I wanted to recognize the strength and merits of the Peruvian case, and at the same time to get appreciation for the Ecuadorian situation, my autonomy, and my role.

My sensitivity to these core concerns helped me navigate this difficult terrain. "President Fujimori," I said, "Peru has a strong claim to the disputed area. Because of the commission's *Parecer*, it may, in fact, be stronger than Ecuador's claim (*appreciating* Peru's point). If I were president of Peru, I'd have no other option than to seek to get every square meter of that land (*appreciating* merit in Peru's perspective).

Yet, as president of Ecuador, I cannot agree to give Peru territory that every president and every Congress since Ecuador was born has insisted is part of Ecuador. (I was asking him to reciprocate by *appreciating* my situation and understanding my difficulties.) We are convinced that we have the moral and legal rights over the area in dispute, and we're not going to change that conviction because of a nonbinding technical opinion (*Parecer*). One hundred more opinions like that one wouldn't be sufficient to change our centuries-old feelings of ownership over those territories. (As a country, we have our *autonomy*.) Hence, any president of Ecuador should say and do what I'm saying and doing. (Asking for his reciprocal *affiliation*.) Now, in our *role* as presidents, we can undertake our new mission, which is to find a formula acceptable for the peoples in both countries." (I was searching for an additional common ground of *affiliation* in fairness and justice.)

This dialogue had the noticeable effect of committing us both to a joint problem-solving approach. Our predominantly rational, carefully prepared, goal-oriented initial steps were additionally fueled by the rapport built rapidly between us and among our delegations. Peace became a flashing beacon, a powerful magnetic force taking up most of our time and energy during my first seventy-seven days in office.

THE AGREEMENT

We kept the people of Ecuador permanently informed about the advance of our negotiation. As progress was evident, a virtuous circle replaced the old vicious one. Negotiation became popular and openly a part of our national objectives. Participation increased. Everybody wanted to be part of the process and to express their voices. Common goals enhanced trust. Political actors started giving support because they understood gains were larger than risks if they represented the now popular will for peace. Belief in a negotiated solution replaced the usual pessimism. Overwhelming support at all levels of society boosted the government's initial action plan. Although this peace process did not stabilize the economy, the menace of war no longer worsened the economic situation.

On October 26, 1998, in Brasilia, ten weeks after our first meeting, President Fujimori and I signed a final, comprehensive peace treaty that was ratified by the Congress of each country. The two countries agreed that the entire disputed boundary area would become an international conservation park in which there would be no economic or military activities except as the two governments might later agree.

Tiwintza itself required special treatment. We two presidents agreed that if the representatives of the four countries that were helping us could concur on a recommendation for Tiwintza, we would commit ourselves to accept it. Congresses of both countries voted to give the representatives authority to arbitrate.

A creative agreement for Tiwintza was formulated. The representatives separated sovereignty rights from property rights over Tiwintza. Thus, the land is now within the sovereign territory of Peru. *And* one square kilometer of land around Tiwintza, just inside Peru and adjoining Ecuador, is now private property owned in perpetuity by the government of Ecuador (just as Ecuador might own some land in Lima, Peru). Neither country "gave up" Tiwintza. The government of Peru can say, "Tiwintza is part of our sovereign territory." The government of Ecuador can say, "We own Tiwintza forever."

A FINAL REFLECTION

I agree with Roger and Dan that negotiators often assume that the best way to negotiate is purely rational. To be sure, strong hostile emotions easily escalate and cause problems. Yet, more importantly, in my experience, emotions can be helpful. When going into negotiations, I was ready to take the initiative and act upon each of the core concerns—on appreciation, affiliation, autonomy, status, and role. In doing so, President Fujimori and I established good rapport, a strong working relationship, and a stable agreement.

The Ecuador-Peru negotiations of 1998 were in themselves a complete success. The boundary was settled and has remained so. Not a single border military incident has been reported since that time. Binational trade and cooperation have reached historical records, and peace has been praised, valued, and owned by governments and citizens alike on both sides of the border.

My major reason for wanting to establish peace between Ecuador and Peru was to give both countries the benefits that only peace could bring. Additionally, establishing peace with Peru would enable Ecuador to reduce its military budget. Those resources could then be devoted to programs to alleviate poverty. And that is what my administration did after the treaty was signed in 1998.

In January 2000, a military-backed coup forced me out of office for reasons too complicated to go into in this document. This fate is one I share with many Latin American presidents.

That is part of the official side of the story. On the personal side, Alberto Fujimori and I gradually developed a personal friendship beyond the call of our duties.

In March 2004, over a cup of coffee in Tokyo's Royal Park Hotel, we reflected on the lessons we learned. Alberto said, "Peace is consolidated. Everybody respects it." In the beginning, few of us believed that peace was possible. Now it was owned by everybody.

Alberto and I remembered a conversation we had in Brazil during the peace process. After a press conference, I had told him: "Things are changing. The situation used to be pretty clear: Ecuadorian journalists on one side, Peruvian journalists on the other. Now they're mixed together. That's a good omen for the future."

Alberto had said, "Yesterday, while reading an article in a Lima newspaper, I felt as if you and I were on the pro-peace side, facing together some opposition to peace in both countries." I nodded in agreement.

Since the beginning, we had worked together to satisfy our core concerns for affiliation, appreciation, and autonomy. Our status was respected. And our roles were fulfilling. We had created an atmosphere to advance substantive content. As almost always happens, process and substance walked hand in hand.

IV

Conclusion

Conclusion

We all have emotions all the time. Yet during a negotiation we have so many things to think about that we give little or no thought to emotions. We become so busy thinking that we let our emotions take care of themselves.

Most negotiators treat emotions as an obstacle to clear, rational thought. As a result, we do not realize the opportunity afforded by positive emotions. Although the Declaration of Independence emphasizes the "pursuit of happiness," there seems to be remarkably little organized common sense about that pursuit.

If we disagree with someone, how can we interact in ways that stimulate positive emotions in both of us? It is against this background that our book advances two big propositions:

First, take the initiative. If you are dealing with someone with whom you disagree, don't wait for emotions to happen and then react.

Second, address the concern, not the emotion. Rather than try to understand every current emotion and its possible causes, focus on five widely shared concerns that can be used to stimulate helpful emotions in others and in you. These core concerns are:

1. **Appreciation.** Feeling unappreciated puts people down. We can appreciate others by *understanding* their point of view; *finding merit* in what they think, feel, or do; and *communicating our understanding* through words or action. We can appreciate ourselves, too.
2. **Affiliation.** Rather than having each negotiator feel alone and disconnected, we can try to build structural connections as colleagues and personal connections as confidantes.
3. **Autonomy.** Recognize that everyone wants freedom to affect or make a great many decisions. We can expand our autonomy and avoid impinging upon theirs.
4. **Status.** No one likes to feel demeaned. Rather than compete with others over who has the higher social status, we can acknowledge everyone's areas of particular status, including our own.
5. **Role.** An unfulfilling role leaves us feeling trivialized and unengaged. Yet we are free to choose roles that help us and others work together. And we can expand the activities within any role to make them fulfilling.

The ideas in this book will not go to work by themselves. It takes a live human being to understand them and put them into practice. You can act in ways that meet the core concerns in others as well as in yourself. Express appreciation. Build a sense of affiliation. Respect each person's autonomy and status. Help shape roles to be fulfilling.

We are confident that using the core concerns wisely will improve the quality of your relationships at work and at home. You can turn a negotiation from a stressful, worrisome interaction into a side-by-side dialogue where each of you listens, learns, and respects the other. You improve your outcome. And instead of inspiring resentment, the process inspires hope.

V

End Matter

End Matter

Seven Elements
of Negotiation

In diagnosing a patient, a medical doctor finds it useful to identify which of the major parts of a body may be causing the symptoms. Is it the digestive system, the circulatory system, the respiratory system, the nervous system, or the skeletal system? Similarly, in diagnosing what may be going wrong with a negotiation, the Harvard Negotiation Project has identified seven elements that comprise the basic anatomy of a negotiation. On page 208 these elements of negotiation are in boldface type down the far left column of the page. For each element, diagnostic questions are suggested in the middle column, and some illustrative prescriptive advice in the right-hand column.

These seven elements form the structure of any negotiation, including "interest-based negotiation," the method described more fully in *Getting to YES: Negotiating Agreement without Giving in,* by Roger Fisher, William Ury, and Bruce Patton (New York: Penguin, 1991). The chart on page 208 does not do *Getting to YES* justice, but it does, we hope, offer you some idea of what that book is about. We also hope the ideas stimulate those of you who have not read the book itself to find the time to do so.

THE SEVEN ELEMENTS:
THE ANATOMY OF A NEGOTIATION

Element	Some Diagnostic Questions	Some Prescriptive Advice
Relationship	How does each negotiator think and feel about the other?	Build rapport and a good working relationship with fellow negotiators. Work together, side by side.
Communication	Is communication poor, deceptive, one way? Are negotiators *telling* one another what to do?	Build easy two-way communication. Inquire, listen, be worthy of trust. Avoid fuzzy promises.
Interests	Are negotiators making demands and stating positions while concealing their true interests that underlie them?	Respect the interests of others. Understand and disclose your own interests. (You need not disclose how *highly* you value what you want.)
Options	Does the negotiation look like a zero-sum game where each side's choice is between winning or losing?	With no commitment, jointly brainstorm possible ways of meeting legitimate interests of both.
Legitimacy	Does no one seem to care about being fair? Are they simply haggling by saying what they are willing or unwilling to do?	Look for and request external standards of fairness that will be persuasive to both.
BATNA (Best Alternative To Negotiated Agreement)	Is each side threatening the other without knowing what they will do if no agreement is reached?	Consider your walk-away alternative as well as theirs. Recognize that any agreement must be better for both than walking away without an agreement.
Commitments	Have negotiators demanded unrealistic commitments from the other side? Have they failed to draft commitments they would be willing to make?	Draft fair and realistic commitments that each side could make.

Glossary

"When I use a word," Humpty Dumpty said, in a rather scornful tone, "it means just what I choose it to mean—neither more nor less."

"The question is," said Alice, "whether you can make words mean so many different things."

"The question is," said Humpty Dumpty, "which is to be master—that's all."

— *THROUGH THE LOOKING GLASS,*
LEWIS CARROLL

Scholars have proposed literally hundreds of definitions for words like emotion. To clarify how we use some of the key terms in this book, we provide a short glossary. There are two sections—one to define emotions and another to define core concerns.

I. WHAT ARE EMOTIONS?

Emotion. An experience to matters of personal significance; typically experienced in association with a distinct type of physical feeling, thought, physiology, and action tendency.

Often a person can choose one emotional response or another, whether to see a rainy day as depressing or as a good day to read a romance novel.

Positive emotions. Uplifting emotions usually resulting from a concern being satisfied. Examples include enthusiasm, hope, and joy. Positive emotions tend to stimulate cooperative action.

Negative emotions. Distressing emotions usually resulting from a concern being unmet. Examples include anger, fear, and guilt. Negative emotions often stimulate competitive action.

Feeling. Used in two ways in this book:

- A *physical sensation*, such as the feeling of hunger or pain
- An *emotion-laden belief*, such as feeling included or appreciated

A feeling (defined as an emotion-laden belief) differs from an emotion in an important way. An emotion is a response that is unarguably true from the perspective of the person experiencing the emotion, regardless of the belief of others. Thus, an emotion is something that we feel and that we are. Anger, for example, can be categorized as an emotion: "I feel angry" is the conceptual equivalent of "I am angry." A feeling, on the other hand, is true from the perspective of the person experiencing the emotion but not necessarily from the perspective of others. Feeling included, for example, fails to meet the criteria of an emotion. A negotiator who feels included may not actually be included by others.

This distinction between an emotion and a feeling holds practical relevance for a negotiator. Because a single feeling often has multiple emotions associated with it, the feeling is pregnant with much more emotional information than any single emotion. Instead of a negotiator having to wade through a huge list of emotion words to identify a person's emotions, that negotiator more easily can use a smaller list of feelings to become aware of a negotiator's emotional experience. In fact, each core concern has a limited set of feelings associated with it. For example, the feelings associated with affiliation range from feeling included to feeling excluded.

Focusing on feelings instead of on emotions risks a loss of precise understanding, but that risk is balanced by the great challenge of any negotiator realistically having the time and attention to become aware of the host of emotions that continually are stirred within any negotiation.

II. WHAT ARE THE CORE CONCERNS?

Core Concern: A human want of personal significance, usually arising within a relationship.

Core concerns are *core* because they touch upon how we want or expect to be treated. A small action affecting a core concern can have a big emotional impact.

There is overlap, but not complete congruence, between the concept of a *core concern* and the concept of a *need* as used by conflict resolution theorists like John Burton and humanistic psychologists like Abraham Maslow. A need is a physiological or psychological requirement for our well-being, such as food or water. No matter if one is negotiating with the president of a country or with a child, a person will still need food, water, and a sense of belonging—and hunger for it if that need goes unmet. A core concern can, perhaps, be considered a more nuanced version of a social need. A core concern usually arises within the context of a relationship and varies in intensity depending upon those with whom one is interacting. A diplomat may experience minimal sensitivity if her child demeans her status but experience great offense if the president of a country demeans that same status.

Appreciation: Used in two ways in this book:

- As a *core concern*, it is a sense of valued recognition.
- As an *action*, it involves understanding someone's point of view; finding merit in their thinking, feeling, or actions; and communicating that understanding.

Affiliation: One's sense of connectedness with another person or group; connections can be structural or personal.

Autonomy: The freedom to affect or make decisions without imposition from others.

Status: One's standing in comparison to the standing of others; *social status* is one's general standing in a social hierarchy, whereas *particular status* is one's standing within some narrowly defined substantive field.

Role: A *job label* and corresponding *set of activities* expected of a person in a specific situation.

Works Consulted

This section provides information on literature that has helped inform our understanding of the emotional dimension of negotiation. The literature on the science of emotion is vast, and this section is not meant to be comprehensive. We have included only those writings that heavily influenced our thinking and those specifically referenced in the text.*

In addition to the literature on the science of emotion, there is a large and growing scientific literature on the specific role of emotion in negotiation. Because that literature is well documented in other places, we have not included most of that research in this section. Some good starting places to learn about cutting-edge research on emotions and negotiation include *The Mind and Heart of the Negotiator* (Leigh Thompson, 3rd ed., Upper Saddle River, NJ: Pearson Prentice Hall, 2005) and *The Handbook of Dispute Resolution* (M. L. Moffitt and R. C. Bordone, eds., San Francisco: Jossey-Bass, 2005).

There are many ways you can use this section. You can read through this entire section to learn more about works related to our core concerns framework. You can get references that peak your interest and read them to keep learning about emotions. If you teach negotiation, you can draw upon some of the resources listed.

---

*For further information on the literature on emotions in negotiation, please write to Daniel Shapiro at the Harvard Negotiation Project, Pound Hall 523, Harvard Law School, Cambridge, MA 02138.

1 EMOTIONS ARE POWERFUL, ALWAYS PRESENT, AND HARD TO HANDLE

What Is an Emotion?

The literature on emotions is complex. To learn more, a good place to start is with a book edited by Paul Ekman and Richard Davidson called *The Nature of Emotion: Fundamental Questions* (Oxford: Oxford University Press, 1994).

To simplify the ideas in our book for practical use, we make no clear distinction between emotions and moods; yet there are differences (e.g., see page 410 of Fiske and Taylor's social psychology classic, *Social Cognition*, 2nd ed., New York: McGraw-Hill, 1991). Compared to moods, emotions generally are seen to be of shorter duration, greater intensity, and greater complexity. As philosophers point out, emotions also have "intentionality"—they are directed toward a specific person or object, whereas the object of a mood usually is more diffuse. For example, you wake up on a Monday morning, find yourself in a grumpy mood, and are irritated at anyone who crosses your path.

The quote illustrating the challenge of defining emotions comes from B. Fehr and J. Russell in their 1984 article, "Concept of Emotion Viewed from a Prototype Perspective," in the *Journal of Experimental Psychology: General*, 113, 464–86.

Emotions Can Be a Great Asset

In 1986, Alice Isen and Peter Carnevale conducted a landmark study showing that a positive mood is associated with creative problem solving in a negotiation ("The Influence of Positive Affect and Visual Access on the Discovery of Integrative Solutions in Bilateral Negotiations," *Organizational Behavior and Human Decision Processes*, 37, 1986, 1–13). For a review of experiments that link positive affect and decision making, see Isen's excellent chapter, "Positive Affect and Decision Making," in the *Handbook of Emotions* (M. Lewis and J. M. Haviland-Jones, eds., 2d ed., New York: Guilford Press, 2000, pp. 417–35).

A new branch of psychology, called "positive psychology," offers evidence that positive emotions enhance rapport, creativity, and social relations. For starters, check out the research of Barbara Fredrickson ("The Role of Positive Emotions in Positive Psychology: The Broaden-and-Build Theory of Positive Emotions," 2001, *American Psychologist*, 56, 218–26).

She suggests that whereas fear, anger, and other negative emotions narrow our attention and prepare us for a specific action (such as to run in fear or fight in anger), positive emotions do just the opposite. They broaden our repertoire of possible actions and thoughts, and they build up reserves we can draw upon when encountering a threat or opportunity. Inspired by Fredrickson's work, Martin Seligman, a past president of the American Psychological Association, proposes that negative emotion evolved to help us in win-lose situations, whereas positive emotions are the basis for successful navigation in win-win interactions (see Martin E. P. Seligman, *Authentic Happiness,* New York: The Free Press, 2002).

The work of Fredrickson and Seligman is consistent with assumptions behind our core concerns framework. We believe that positive emotions stimulate a variety of helpful effects, including rapport, good relations, openness, friendliness, and creativity—all of which make it easier to create a mutually satisfying agreement.

A great deal of research has emerged on the power of "emotional intelligence." For background, we refer you to the work of P. Salovey and J. Mayer (e.g., 1990, "Emotional Intelligence," *Imagination, Cognition, and Personality,* 9, 185–211) and D. Goleman (*Emotional Intelligence,* New York: Bantam, 1995).

We illustrated the power of positive emotions using Carter's negotiation with Begin and Sadat. That example is drawn from Carter's book *Keeping Faith: Memoirs of a President* (Fayetteville, AK: The University of Arkansas Press, 1995, pp. 298, 318, 350, 408, and 412). William Quandt describes Carter's and Begin's relationship in less positive terms, at times characterized by mistrust and irritation (see his book *Camp David: Peacemaking and Politics,* Washington, D.C.: Brookings Institution, 1986, p. 184). He attributes the success of Camp David in great part to Carter's perseverance and optimism as well as to his good relationship with Sadat, whom Carter both liked and admired (p. 258). In *Keeping Faith,* Carter himself acknowledged that there was some tension in his relationship with Begin. These hurdles, however, did not prevent Carter from using emotions to create as positive an environment and relationship as possible.

Stop Having Emotions? You Can't.

Daniel Shapiro suggests that we are in a state of "perpetual emotion" during social interactions ("A Negotiator's Guide to Emotion: Four Laws to

Effective Practice," *Dispute Resolution Magazine,* Vol. 18, #6, September 2001), and studies in social psychology offer supporting evidence. For example, John Bargh has conducted innovative research showing that we have automatic emotional reactions—often without even being consciously aware of those reactions (e.g., J. A. Bargh and T. L. Chartrand [1999], "The Unbearable Automaticity of Being," *American Psychologist, 54* [7], 462–79).

While we suggest that a person cannot stop having emotions, there are exceptions. For example, feelings may be absent from individuals with particular kinds of brain damage. Such a condition can reduce effective decision making. Antonio Damasio describes a case where a brain-damaged patient lacking emotion spent half an hour deciding when next to meet Damasio. He lacked a gut feeling to help him decide. (See Antonio Damasio's excellent book *Descartes' Error: Emotion, Reason, and the Human Brain,* London: Picador, 1995.)

Ignore Emotions? It Won't Work.

Research suggests a clear link between emotion and thinking, physiological change, and behavior. Consider the concept of an "action tendency," developed by Nico Fridja (*The Emotions,* Cambridge: Cambridge University Press, 1986). An action tendency is the kind of behavior that an emotion directs us to do. Fear gets our body and mind ready to run. Anger gets us ready to fight. We may not follow through with the tendency, but our body and mind prepare us to do so. Thus, an emotion affects us whether we like it or not.

Admittedly, ignoring an emotion can be helpful under certain conditions, such as when we receive a birthday gift from a colleague and do not like it. But even when we suppress emotions, they still tend to have an impact on our mental functioning (e.g., see E. A. Butler and J. J. Gross, "Hiding Feelings in Social Contexts: Out of Sight Is Not Out of Mind," in P. Philippot and R. S. Feldman, eds., *The Regulation of Emotion,* Mahwah, NJ: Erlbaum, 2004, pp. 101–26). Emotions consume mental resources, affect the cardiovascular system in ways that appear to be out of sync with metabolic demand, and even can lead to increased blood pressure in one's social partner (see "Wise Emotion Regulation," by J. Gross and O. John, in Barrett and Salovey, eds., *Wisdom of Feelings,* New York: Guilford Press, 2002, pp. 312–13).

Deal Directly with Emotions?

Some emotion researchers believe there are dozens of emotions while others offer evidence for a limited set of "basic emotions." (For perspectives on what constitutes a "basic" emotion, see Ekman and Davidson's edited book, cited earlier.)

Paul Ekman is a pioneer in the study of basic emotions. He views basic emotions as having evolutionary roots and an adaptive function for survival. He proposes a list of fifteen emotions that are distinct from one another and that meet his criteria for what constitutes a basic emotion ("Basic Emotions," in T. Dalgleish and T. Power, eds., *The Handbook of Cognition and Emotion*, Sussex, UK: John Wiley & Sons, 1999, pp. 45–60). He notes that the actual number of emotions is greatly expanded, because each basic emotion actually denotes a family of related emotions.

This helps explain why, in *Beyond Reason*, we have chosen to focus on five core concerns. One need not analyze which of the various emotions the other person is feeling, nor their causes, in order to use the core concerns to enlist positive emotions. Rather than focusing on dozens of emotions, a negotiator can take action with five core concerns.

Nevertheless, the more emotionally attuned a negotiator is, the more effectively he or she will be able to calibrate his or her behavior. Having skill in recognizing facial expressions or reading another's emotions is thus of significant value (see D. Goleman's book and the article by Salovey and Mayer, cited earlier) as long as the negotiator is not overwhelmed with the task and loses focus on relational or substantive matters.

Where do we stand on the question of whether there are "basic emotions"? We believe that there may be a subset of evolutionarily determined basic emotions, but that there is a large subset of socially meaningful, qualitatively unique emotional experiences. Anger, for example, is different in experience and effect than annoyance, rage, or humiliation. On page 13, we provided an illustrative list of fifty emotions, many of which are extracted from the classic emotion text by Richard Lazarus, *Emotion and Adaptation* (Oxford: Oxford University Press, 1991).

2 ADDRESS THE CONCERN, NOT THE EMOTION

Five Core Concerns Stimulate Many Emotions

Years back, Charles Horton Cooley proposed the notion of the "looking glass self," suggesting that our understanding of ourselves—our identity—is based on how we perceive that others see us (*Human Nature and the Social Order*, New York: Charles Scribner's Sons, 1902). The core concerns framework recognizes this fundamental insight.

In the research literature, Daniel Shapiro refers to the core concerns as "relational identity concerns." He has developed theory clarifying the connection between emotions and relational identity concerns. (For details, see D. L. Shapiro, "Negotiating Emotions," *Conflict Resolution Quarterly*, 2002; 20 [1]: 67–82. Also see D. L. Shapiro, "Enemies, Allies, and Emotions: The Role of Emotions in Negotiation," in M. Moffitt and R. Bordone, eds., *The Handbook of Dispute Resolution*, 2005.)

Use the Core Concerns as a Lens

Our core concerns framework is congruent with many emotion theories. Consider the work of Lazarus and Ekman. Lazarus proposes that we evaluate our interactions for "core relational themes," generalized relational meanings about an interaction (*Emotion and Adaptation*, Oxford: Oxford University Press, 1991, p. 121). As he states, core relational themes are the "central (hence core) relational harm or benefit in adaptational encounters that underlies each specific kind of emotion." From this theoretical perspective, then, core concerns may be considered relational themes that emerge within many, if not most, interactions; how we evaluate treatment of our core concerns manifests as an emotion.

Ekman similarly suggests that we have "autoappraisers" that continually scan for "themes and variations of the events that have been relevant for our survival" (*Emotions Revealed: Recognizing Faces and Feelings to Improve Communication and Emotional Life*, New York: Henry Holt, 2003, p. 29). When these autoappraisers find a relevant theme or variation, emotions are called forth. Autoappraisers, then, may be "programmed" to survey our interactions for signs that core concerns are met or unmet. There clearly has been evolutionary importance in affiliating with the right group, having enough autonomy to protect ourselves from harm, and having a social status that does not threaten others who can hurt or kill us. Emotions notify us of the result of this process.

Use the Core Concerns as a Lever

Although you can use the core concerns proactively to set the emotional tone you want, what happens if the other person is in a bad mood? There is evidence that you can overwhelm—or "undo"—the effects of negative emotions with positive ones (e.g., see B. Fredrickson and R. Levenson, 1998, "Positive Emotions Speed Recovery from the Cardiovascular Sequelae of Negative Emotions," *Cognition and Emotion,* 12 [2], 191–220).

Furthermore, emotions are contagious (e.g., E. Hatfield, J. T. Cacioppo, and R. L. Rapson, 1993, "Emotional Contagion," in *Current Directions in Psychological Science,* 2 [3], 96–99). We sometimes "catch" the mood of another, and often this effect occurs outside our conscious awareness. Talking with a depressed person can make us sad while seeing a baby smile may bring an automatic smile to our face. Emotional contagion provides us with an opportunity: We can enlist positive emotions in ourselves, making it more likely that the other negotiator will catch our enthusiasm.

3 EXPRESS APPRECIATION:
FIND MERIT IN WHAT OTHERS THINK
FEEL, OR DO—AND SHOW IT

Appreciation: A Core Concern and an All-Purpose Action

If you want to learn more about the power of appreciation, we highly recommend you look into the research and writing of John Gottman, a professor in the Department of Psychology at the University of Washington in Seattle. For many years, he and colleagues have studied one of the most challenging social relationships—that between marital partners (see J. Gottman and N. Silver, *The Seven Principles for Making Marriage Work,* New York: Three Rivers Press, 1999).

He brings newlyweds into his "love lab" and hooks them up to all kinds of devices to record their physiology, facial expressions, words, and the extent to which they wiggle in their chair. He asks the couple to spend fifteen minutes discussing a disagreement between them. Afterward, he reviews the interaction on videotape with each partner independently and asks each what emotions were felt.

He is able to predict—apparently with more than 90 percent accuracy—which couples will get divorced several years down the road. And a key factor in divorce is the failure of couples to appreciate one another. In stable marriages, the ratio of positive to negative moment-to-moment interactions is five to one during a disagreement. Partners share at least five positive interactions—smiling, appreciating one another, or making a friendly joke—to counter every biting comment, condescending remark, or demeaning eye rolling. In unstable marriages, the ratio is closer to one positive interaction for every one negative interaction.

Gottman's research supports our notion that there is great power in initiating a positive tone to a negotiation (J. M. Gottman, J. Coan, S. Carrere, and C. Swanson, "Predicting Marital Happiness and Stability from Newlywed Interactions," *Journal of Marriage and the Family*, 60, 1998, 5–22). In 96 percent of the cases he studied, a conversation that started on a positive tone maintained a positive tone; a conversation that began negatively tended to stay negative. Thus, these findings offer evidence that even in ongoing relationships, setting a positive tone to a negotiation can improve the emotional tenor of the entire discussion.

Gottman's research also underscores *Building Agreement* focus on core concerns and not on emotions per se. The complexity of Gottman's research paradigm is almost as impressive as his results. In order to get a good sense of what each marital partner is experiencing, he extracts an incredible amount of data, from facial expression to blood pressure, sweat level to body language. The data he gathers are analyzed by sophisticated mathematics and computer technology. In a negotiation, it would be extremely difficult to focus on substantive and procedural issues while simultaneously observing for all the data points he records.

Additional research on the power of appreciation comes from the Institute of HeartMath. Their studies reveal that a sustained state of appreciation is associated with improved cognitive ability and performance. They have noted that physiological coherence—a pattern of increased synchronization between the heart, brain, and related physiological systems—rarely occurs for sustained periods of time. An exception, they found, happens when a person is in a state of sincere appreciation. As a result, there is reduced anxiety and stress symptoms, improved cognitive performance, and decreases in cortisol. (See R. McCraty and D. Childre, "The Grateful Heart: The Psychophysiology of Appreciation," in R. A. Emmons and M. E. McCullough, eds., *The Psychology of Gratitude,* New York: Oxford University Press, 2004, pp. 230–55.)

Three Elements to Express Appreciation

Our notion of appreciation is closely aligned to Carl Rogers's idea of "empathic understanding," a process of listening actively and without judgment to a person's emotions, values, and views. Rogers suggests that we listen to another's point of view as if our own, in essence trying to see the merit and legitimacy in that point of view. He also suggests the importance of communicating our understanding of the other's point of view—and checking its accuracy—through paraphrasing. (See C. Rogers, *On Becoming a Person*, Boston: Houghton Mifflin, 1961.)

Listen for Meta-Messages

The observation that we have emotions about emotions goes back at least as far as 1964, when Tomkins and McCarter discussed "affect-about-affect" (see "What and Where Are the Primary Affects? Some Evidence for a Theory," *Perception Motor Skills*, 18, 119–58). For practical information on meta-messages, we refer the reader to chapter 5 of the excellent book *Messages: The Communication Skills Book* (M. McKay, M. Davis, and P. Fanning, Oakland, CA: New Harbinger Publications, 1995).

Try the Role Reversal Exercise

The role reversal exercise is a process for stepping into the other negotiator's shoes, thus helping us to overcome the "fundamental attribution error" (a term coined by Stanford psychologist Lee Ross). The fundamental attribution error suggests that when we judge someone, we tend to overweigh the "kind of" person he or she is and to underweigh the social pressures affecting that person. Consequently, we risk making errors in explaining the cause of the person's behavior. We may think that the other negotiator's rude behavior is a product of his rude disposition, when in fact he is a typically tempered individual who unfortunately got into a big fight this morning with his spouse. (For details on the fundamental attribution error, see L. Ross, "The Intuitive Psychologist and His Shortcomings: Distortions in the Attribution Process," in L. Berkowitz, ed., *Advances in Experimental Social Psychology*, vol. 10, New York: Academic Press, 1977.)

4 BUILD AFFILIATION: TURN AN ADVERSARY INTO A COLLEAGUE

In social psychology, Baumeister and Leary reviewed research on the "need to belong" (R. Baumeister and M. Leary, "The Need to Belong: Desire for Interpersonal Attachments as a Fundamental Human Motivation," in *Psychological Bulletin*, 1995, 117[3], 497–529). Based upon their extensive review of the scientific literature, they conclude that:

- there exists a fundamental motive to bond;

- people bond even without material advantage;

- strong negative emotions correlate with broken bonds;

- stable bonds produce positive emotions and opium-like chemicals in the brain; and

- people without stable bonds tend to suffer higher levels of mental and physical illness and are more prone to behavioral problems ranging from traffic accidents to suicide.

In neuroscience, evidence reveals a link between broken bonds and negative emotions. Naomi Eisenberger and colleagues have shown that the pain of social rejection registers in the same part of the brain as physical pain (i.e., in the anterior cingulate cortex). The study suggests that "social pain is analogous in its neurocognitive function to physical pain, alerting us when we have sustained injury to our social connections, allowing restorative measures to be taken." (N. Eisenberger, M. Lieberman, and K. Williams, "Does Rejection Hurt? An fMRI Study of Social Exclusion," *Science,* vol. 302, October 10, 2003.)

Structural Connection

Favoritism toward "our own group" is created in even the most minimal of conditions. In one study, participants were told that they had been randomly assigned to a group. They were even shown the lottery ticket that determined to which group they would belong. Despite the meaningless classification of participants, they showed a preference for members of their own group. (See A. Locksley, V. Ortiz, and C. Hepburn, 1980, "Social Categorization and

Discriminatory Behavior: Extinguishing the Minimal Intergroup Discrimination Effect," *Journal of Personality and Social Psychology,* 39 [5], 773–83. Also see M. Billig and H. Tajfel, 1973, "Social Categorization and Similarity in Intergroup Behavior," *European Journal of Social Psychology,* 3 [1] 27–52.)

Tajfel has further developed the notion of "social identity theory," suggesting that people in a group seek to boost their self-esteem by positively differentiating their group from a comparison group on a valued dimension. People's identity becomes wrapped up in their group membership. (See H. Tajfel and J. C. Turner, "The Social Identity Theory of Inter-Group Behavior," in S. Worchel and W. G. Austin, eds., *Psychology of Intergroup Relations,* Chicago: Nelson-Hall, 1986.)

Kurt Lewin, a pioneer in social psychology, conducted a study that illustrates the power of structural connections ("Group Decision and Social Change," in T. M. Newcomb and E. L. Hartley, eds., *Readings in Social Psychology,* New York: Henry Holt, 1947). One of his classic studies, conducted during World War II, investigated factors that would persuade housewives to serve intestinal meat. In one condition, housewives attended a lecture on the wartime and health benefits of serving the meat. Afterward, only 3 percent of the housewives reported serving it. In a second condition, a different group of women was invited into a discussion on whether "housewives like themselves" could be induced to serve intestinal meat. Afterward, nearly one third of the participants served the meat. The structural connection of being "housewives" and offering support to "housewives like themselves" apparently boosted their willingness to serve the meat.

Personal Connection

Building personal connections takes work. We feel closer, then more distant, then closer again. It is hard to maintain an optimal emotional distance, as exemplified by the porcupine example from chapter four, which we derived from a fable written by Arthur Schopenhauer in *Parerga and Paralipomena: Short Philosophical Essays,* 4th ed., vol. ii § 396 (Oxford: Clarendon Press, 1974). See the research of Baxter to learn more about this tension between being open versus closed (e.g., see L. Baxter, "A Dialectical Perspective on Communication Strategies in Relationship Development," in S. Duck, ed., *Handbook of Personal Relationships: Theory, Research, and Interventions,* Chichester, UK: Wiley, 1988, pp. 257–73).

5 RESPECT AUTONOMY: EXPAND YOURS (AND DON'T IMPINGE UPON THEIRS)

What Is Autonomy?

To learn more about research and theory on autonomy, check out the work of Edward Deci (*The Psychology of Self-Determination,* Lexington, MA: Lexington Books, 1980). He suggests that the "will" is our capacity to choose how to satisfy our needs. Self-determination (or "autonomy" in the language of *Building Agreement*) involves utilizing that will.

Expand Your Autonomy

Research reveals that we sometimes underestimate the degree of autonomy we do have. When we fail repeatedly at a task, we may become emotionally paralyzed and passive. Experiments demonstrate that people become depressed when they feel they have no control over their destiny (M. Seligman, *Helplessness: On Depression, Development, and Death,* 2d ed., San Francisco: W. H. Freeman, 1991). In other words, they lack a sense of autonomy over their lives.

"Learned helplessness" occurs when we accept miserable life conditions despite having autonomy to improve our situation. We learn to be helpless. Learned helplessness was first observed in experiments in which animals were electrically shocked and harnessed to prevent escape. When released from the harness and given the opportunity to avoid the shock, many passively accepted the shock (M. Seligman, and G. Beagley, 1975, "Learned Helplessness in the Rat," *Journal of Comparative and Physiological Psychology,* 88 [2], 534–41).

Albert Bandura approaches the issue of autonomy from a related perspective. His research on "self-efficacy" suggests that the more we think we can do, the more we can do (A. Bandura, *Self-Efficacy: The Exercise of Control,* New York: Freeman, 1997). The belief that we are competent and capable to accomplish a task—whether a math problem or a difficult negotiation—enhances our performance, motivation, and commitment to the task.

Don't Impinge upon Their Autonomy

Research reveals that if someone impinges upon our autonomy, we may experience "psychological reactance" (J. Brehm, *A Theory of Psychological Reactance,* New York: Academic Press, 1966). This often happens when we think we have multiple choices about how to act—and then someone eliminates or threatens to eliminate one of those choices. Now we may want to engage in that behavior more than before!

Use the I-C-N Bucket System

The Bucket System was developed by Mark Gordon, a senior advisor to the Harvard Negotiation Project. For similar approaches on deciding how to decide, see *Leadership and Decision-Making* by Victor Vroom and Philip Yetton, Pittsburgh: University of Pittsburgh Press, 1973; also see *Power Up,* by David Bradford and Allan Cohen, New York: John Wiley & Sons, Inc., 1998.

6 ACKNOWLEDGE STATUS: RECOGNIZE HIGH STANDING WHEREVER DESERVED

Status Can Enhance Our Esteem and Influence

A number of theorists suggest that we are driven to seek status. Years ago, Alfred Adler proposed that each of us is born with an inferior sense of status. We are young. Our parents are older and wiser. Over time, excessive inferiority can turn into an "inferiority complex." To overcome feelings of inferiority, Adler suggested that we have a "striving for superiority," which drives our thoughts, actions, and emotions (*The Education of Children,* Chicago: Allen and Unwin, 1930).

Adler's theory foreshadowed contemporary research on emotion. Kemper has found a link between status and emotion (T. Kemper, "Social Models in the Explanation of Emotions," in Michael Lewis and Jeannette M. Haviland-Jones, eds., *Handbook of Emotions,* 2d ed., New York: The Guilford Press, 2004). And John Gottman's marital work demonstrates the particular toxicity of the emotion of contempt on the health of a marriage (see *Why Marriages Succeed or Fail . . . and How You Can Make Yours Last,* New York: Simon & Schuster, 1995). As Nico Frijda notes, "Contempt consists of the appraisal of a person as being of such low value as to be disqualified for entering into social interaction as an equal to oneself, while at the same time perceiving that person's presumption to be equal" (in "Emotions and Action," in *Feelings and Emotions: The Amsterdam Symposium*, Antony S. R. Manstead, Nico Frijda, and Agneta Fischer, eds., Cambridge: University of Cambridge, 2004, pp. 167–68).

There Is No Need to Compete over Status

Our notion of "multiple areas of status" has roots in the work of Adam Smith. He theorized that individual welfare can benefit by having people specialize in a specific area and then make exchanges with others who have different specialties. (See Adam Smith, *An Inquiry into the Nature and Causes of the Wealth of Nations*, London: Methuen and Co., 1776.) In a negotiation, each person can benefit from the areas of particular expertise or experience of the other.

Know the Limits of Status

A number of studies illustrate the concept we term "status spillover." For example, check out the work of Cohen and David, who provide case studies and discussion of medical mistakes resulting from a person following—without question—the orders of a perceived higher status individual, even when the orders are illogical (M. Cohen and N. Davis, *Medication Errors: Causes and Prevention*, Philadelphia: G. F. Stickley Co., 1981).

7 CHOOSE A FULFILLING ROLE— AND SELECT THE ACTIVITIES WITHIN IT

We suggest that a fulfilling role is not acting or pretense. This was evident in the negotiation between Lord Caradon and Deputy Foreign Minister Kuznetsov over UN Resolution 242. Information on that example comes from two sources. Lord Caradon wrote about his experience in the fascinating book *U.N. Security Council Resolution 242: A Case Study in Diplomatic Ambiguity*, Lord Caradon, Arthur Goldberg, Mohamed El-Zayyat, and Abba Eban, Washington, D.C.: Institute for the Study of Diplomacy, Edmund A. Walsh School of Foreign Service, Georgetown University, 1981. Elements of the story also are based upon personal conversations between Roger Fisher and Lord Caradon.

Our notion of a "fulfilling role" connects closely with the work of Viktor Frankl. In his book *Man's Search for Meaning,* he describes how, despite being in a concentration camp in Nazi Germany, he was able to find meaning in his experience (New York: Simon & Schuster, 1984). He proposes that we have a "will to meaning," the striving to find and fulfill meaning and purpose in our lives.

A fulfilling role also helps you feel in the "flow" with the task in which you are engaged. Here our thinking was influenced by Mihalyi Csikszentmihalyi, who has researched the experience of "flow" (*Flow: The Psychology of Optimal Experience,* New York: Harper & Row, 1990). He states that flow is "the state in which people are so involved in an activity that nothing else seems to matter; the experience itself is so enjoyable that people will do it at great cost, for the sheer sake of doing it" (page 4).

8 ON STRONG NEGATIVE EMOTIONS: THEY HAPPEN. BE READY.

To demonstrate the problems of strong emotions in a negotiation, we opened the chapter with an example about Burger Brothers. This example is based upon a comparable situation at a Fortune 500 company in a different business sector. The names of individuals and the company, as well as the context of the example, have been changed to preserve people's confidentiality.

As described in chapter 1, observing for every emotion as it happens would be difficult for a negotiator. Research shows, however, that people are fairly good at recognizing the expression of strong emotions (see page 76 of Ekman's book *Emotions Revealed,* New York: Henry Holt, 2003). Because strong negative emotions offer a unique set of challenges for a negotiator, this chapter describes a distinct approach for dealing with strong emotions.

Strong Negative Emotions Can Sidetrack a Negotiation

Daniel Shapiro uses the term "vertigo" to describe the cognitive narrowing and emotionally "dizzying" effect of strong emotion upon one's experience. For a book chapter applying the concept to conflict resolution, see D. L. Shapiro and V. Liu, "The Psychology of a Stable Peace" in M. Fitzduff and C. Stout, eds., *The Psychology of Resolving Global Conflicts: From War to Peace,* 2005.

To learn more about the role of negative emotions on your social interactions, read Daniel Goleman's book *Emotional Intelligence* (cited earlier); in this book, he explains how our "emotional brain" (the amygdala) can override our "thinking brain" (the neocortex).

Have an Emergency Plan Ready Before Negative Emotions Arise

Recently, Joseph LeDoux made a landmark discovery about the neuropsychology of emotion (see *The Emotional Brain: The Mysterious Underpinnings of Emotional Life,* London: Weidenfeld & Nicolson, 1998). When information enters your brain via your eyes and ears, it does not always travel first to your "thinking brain." The information is first "sorted" by a part of your brain called the thalamus. If your thalamus recognizes emotional information—such as if your immediate physical safety is in jeopardy—it immediately signals your emotional brain. As a result, you begin to react emotionally before you have time to deliberate on your situation. You automatically jump back toward safety if you see a snake coiled and ready to bite you. Yet when information goes first to your emotional brain, you may end up saying or doing something you later regret.

When emotions are strong, there is often a period during which the emotion still affects us even though the problem has been managed. After seeing a snake and jumping back, you still may feel anxious for an hour or two. After getting into an argument with a family member, you may feel upset even after you resolved the conflict.

A strong emotion and its residual effect hinder our ability to access information that contradicts the emotion's related thoughts, feelings, and action tendency. Upon dissolution of the residual effect, we become more able to see our situation in a new light. Thus, we suggest soothing techniques or a break if emotions heat up.

Soothe Yourself and Others

For well-researched information on a mind/body approach to relaxation, read the work of Herbert Benson. Start with his classic book, *The Relaxation Response* (H. Benson with M. Klipper, HarperCollins: New York, 2000).

Know Your Purpose

A great deal of research reveals the limitations of venting. For more information, we refer you to Eileen Kennedy-Moore and Jeanne C. Watson's book, *Expressing Emotion: Myths, Realities, and Therapeutic Strategies* (New York: Guilford Press, 1999) and Carol Tavris's book *Anger: The Misunderstood Emotion* (New York: Simon & Schuster, 1989).

Strong negative emotions often erupt when we are faced with a difficult conversation. While writing *Building Agreement,* we were fortunate to receive insight from colleagues who wrote *Difficult Conversations: How to Discuss What Matters Most* (Douglas Stone, Bruce Patton, and Sheila Heen, New York: Viking, 2000). Their book offers advice to manage three layers to a difficult conversation: the content, the feelings, and the identity-related issues.

ADDENDUM

Here is a sampling of the many resources available to learn more about negotiation. Roger Fisher, William Ury, and Bruce Patton describe the steps of interest-based negotiation in *Getting to YES: Negotiating Agreement without Giving In* (New York: Penguin, 1991). Bruce Patton describes the "Seven Elements of Negotiation" in a chapter called "Negotiation," in *The Handbook of Dispute Resolution,* M. L. Moffitt and R. C. Bordone, eds. (San Francisco: Jossey-Bass, 2005). Leigh L. Thompson offers an overview of research on negotiation in *The Mind and Heart of the Negotiator* (3rd ed., Upper Saddle River, NJ: Pearson Prentice Hall, 2005). Max Bazerman and Margaret Neale describe common errors made by negotiators, and provide prescriptive advice to avoid such errors (see *Negotiating Rationally,* New York: Free Press, 1993).

For negotiations involving agents, such as those that often occur in law and business, Robert Mnookin, Scott Peppet, and Andrew Tulumello offer a negotiation framework of the "three tensions" that occur in a negotiation: between principal and agent, empathy and assertion, and creating and distributing value (see *Beyond Winning: Negotiating to Create Value in Deals and Disputes,* Cambridge, MA: Belknap Press of Harvard University Press, 2000). Deborah Kolb examines negotiation through a gender lens (see her book jointly written with Judith Williams, *Everyday Negotiation: Navigating*

Works Consulted

the Hidden Agendas in Bargaining, San Francisco: Jossey-Bass, 2003). Lax and Sebenius develop negotiation theory and advice in *The Manager as Negotiator: Bargaining for Cooperation and Competitive Gain* (D. Lax and J. Sebenius, New York: Free Press, 1986). If you want to learn about consensus building, check out *Consensus Building Handbook: A Comprehensive Guide to Reaching Agreement* (L. Susskind, S. McKearnan, and J. Thomas-Larmer, Thousand Oaks, CA: Sage Publications, 1999). For an analytical approach to negotiation, read *Negotiation Analysis: The Science and Art of Collaborative Decision Making* (Howard Raiffa with John Richardson and David Metcalfe, Cambridge, MA: Belknap Press, 2003). For a recent review of the negotiation literature, read "Negotiation" (M. H. Bazerman, J. R. Curhan, D. A. Moore, and K. L. Valley, 2000, *Annual Review of Psychology, 51,* 279–314).

For an overview of conflict resolution, see *The Handbook of Conflict Resolution: Theory and Practice,* Morton Deutsch and Peter Coleman, eds. (San Francisco: Jossey-Bass, 2000). For an examination of multiple forms of dispute resolution, try *Dispute Resolution: Beyond the Adversarial Model* (Carrie J. Menkel-Meadow, Lela Porter Love, Andrea Kupfer Schneider, and Jean R. Sternlight, Aspen, CO: Aspen Publishing, 2004). A widely used negotiation textbook is *Essentials of Negotiation* (Roy J. Lewicki, Bruce Barry, David M. Saunders and John W. Minton, 3rd ed. New York: McGraw-Hill, 2003).

Acknowledgments

Working on this book day to day has been an adventure in camaraderie. Our colleagues at the Harvard Negotiation Project have been indispensable. Bruce Patton, Sheila Heen, and Doug Stone spent hours talking with us, challenging our ideas, and applying their expertise from writing *Difficult Conversations: How to Discuss What Matters Most*.

Linda Kluz, administrative assistant at the Harvard Negotiation Project, dedicated endless hours to help this project move forward and to make sure that all of us stayed sane as writing deadlines approached.

We feel privileged to have a professional home at the Program on Negotiation based at Harvard Law School (PON). Bob Mnookin, professor of law at Harvard Law School and chair of PON, has embraced the cutting-edge philosophy of PON by supporting initiatives such as ours. He has offered helpful insights and has been instrumental in promoting our course at Harvard Law School, "Negotiation: Dealing with Emotions." Thank you, Bob. And thank you, Dean Elena Kagan, for the Harvard Law School's support of our work on the emotional dimension of negotiation.

Our other PON colleagues and friends have offered useful insights and ideas. We wish to thank (in alphabetical order): Max Bazerman, professor at Harvard Business School, who challenged our thinking early on and helped us to clarify our framework; Eric Berger of the Kennedy School of Government, who spent hours exploring ideas with us; Bob Bordone, lecturer on law at Harvard Law School (and lecturer extraordinaire), who has been a daily source of encouragement, inspiration, and friendship; Bill Breslin, former editor of the *Negotiation Journal;* Sara Cobb, to whom we owe a great debt of gratitude for supporting this project from its inception during her tenure as executive director of PON; Jared Curhan, assistant professor at the Sloan School of Management, MIT, for his collegiality and innovative research on "subjective value"; and Ehud Eiran, expert on Israeli politics with whom we consulted on the Camp David example in Chapter One.

Other PON colleagues we wish to thank include Susan Hackley, managing director of PON, who has been a daily source of inspiration and wisdom; James Kerwin, assistant director of PON, for the many helpful brainstorming sessions; Astrid Kleinhanns, former fellow at PON; Tom Kochan, professor at MIT Sloan; Debbie Kolb, professor at Simmons College, whose work on negotiation informed our thinking; Melissa Manwaring, director of curriculum development at PON, for her creative input and colleagueship; Howard Raiffa, professor emeritus at Harvard, with gratitude to a negotiation trailblazer; Mary Rowe, MIT ombudsperson and adjunct professor of negotiation, who has been teaching MIT Sloan students about emotional intelligence since long before the term was coined; Bob McKersie, professor emeritus at MIT Sloan, whose expertise we drew upon regarding the labor-management example in *Building Agreement;* and Jeswald Salacuse, professor at the Fletcher School of Law and Diplomacy at Tufts University, for our lunchtime conversations about how to teach the interpersonal dimension of negotiation.

Additional PON faculty we would like to thank include Frank Sander, professor at Harvard Law School, for his penetrating questions that stirred our thinking; Jim Sebenius, professor at Harvard Business School, whose ideas on negotiation sequencing influenced how we approached Chapter Nine on preparation; Larry Susskind, professor at MIT, for his support and negotiation insights; Liz Tippett, whose desk sits adjacent to our offices: thank you for putting up with our daily requests and always with a thoughtful response; Mike

Wheeler, professor at Harvard Business School, whose work on improvisation and negotiation has inspired our thinking; Bill Ury, director of the Global Negotiation Project, who shares a similar vision of how we can make a difference in this world; and Josh Weiss, associate director of the Global Negotiation Project, for the countless times he has answered our questions.

A special thank-you to the participants and organizers of Harvard Law School's monthly Dispute Resolution Forum as well as to the staff at PON: Rob Bosso, Ed Hillis, Nancy Lawton, Ron Monteverde, Adam Motenko, Nancy Waters, and Kim Wright. You keep PON radiant.

Comments from many psychologists have been crucial to the development of *Building Agreement*. The work of Keith Allred, associate professor at the Kennedy School of Government and a colleague at PON, contributed to our thinking. Susan Fiske, professor at Princeton University, helped Dan formulate his empirical research on the role of emotions in negotiation. Kimberlyn Leary, director of psychology at Cambridge Hospital/Harvard Medical School and a colleague at PON, has a wonderful sense of how people's emotional lives "work," and she applied her rigorous psychoanalytic insight to her feedback. Phil Levendusky, director of psychology at McLean Hospital/Harvard Medical School, is a born negotiator and offered his suggestions through the lens of cognitive behavioral psychology. Steve Nisenbaum, senior psychologist at Massachusetts General Hospital and on the faculty at Harvard Medical School, is a Massachusetts legend as mediator; he shared with us his rigorous thinking and warmth of friendship. Bruce Shackleton, also on Harvard Medical School's faculty, provided a wealth of ideas on the role of emotions in negotiation.

Additionally, few people in the world could offer the kind of feedback given by Hal Movius of the Consensus Building Institute and Rebecca Wolfe of Princeton University; through their expertise in both emotion theory and negotiation theory, they noted important areas of our book that needed revising or referencing.

We are grateful to Howard Gardner, professor at Harvard's

School of Education, with whom we discussed connections between his theories and ours. Jerome Kagan of the Harvard Psychology Department offered ideas on a definition of emotions. A special thanks to our Romanian colleagues, Ruxandra Tudose and Veronica Bogorin, mental health specialists. We fondly remember the conversations with you and your colleagues at Babej Boyes University, and we have integrated many of your suggestions into this book.

Colleagues who teach negotiation and leadership in the public and private sector reviewed drafts. Longtime colleagues Ueli Egger and Frits Philips provided valuable input based on their years of experience as top negotiation consultants in Europe. Mark Gordon, a partner at Vantage Partners (a negotiation consulting firm), has been available at any time for feedback, even amid his busy traveling schedule, and he graciously lent us the concept of the "Bucket System" that we describe in Chapter Five. John Richardson, a longtime colleague at the Harvard Negotiation Project, never failed to provide a fresh view on our ideas and to illuminate unstated assumptions. Tom Schaub of CMPartners carefully reviewed a draft of this book in light of his years of conflict resolution consulting and helped us solidify some of the terms; and Jim Tull brought to bear his years of international experience as a negotiation consultant. Wayne Davis helped us locate information on our example involving United Nations Resolution 242. The ever-insightful Marty Linsky of Harvard's Kennedy School of Government read drafts of the manuscript and offered advice on how we could clarify our ideas.

For the past several years, we have taught a course at Harvard Law School based on the evolving concepts in this book. We hope our students learned nearly as much from us as we did from them. We also are grateful for feedback from students and teaching assistants involved in Dan's negotiation courses at the Sloan School of Management, Massachusetts Institute of Technology.

We marvel at the dedication and intellectual talent of our student research assistants. In addition to their heavy workloads at Harvard, they somehow managed to devote hour upon hour of time and enthusiasm to our project, working much beyond the call of duty. Thank you Maria Anzorreguy, David Baharvar, Shana Becker,

Brooke Clayton, Susie Goodman, Emily Howard, Audrey Lee, Joe Nuccio, Catherine O'Gorman, Hansel Pham, Zoe Siegler-Reichlin, Emma Waring, and Hanna Weiss.

There were many others who helped with the development of this book. We learned from Michael Cohen at Harvard Medical School, Marjorie Corman Aaron of the University of Cincinnati Law School, Jeff Francois at the Kennedy School of Government, Clark Freshman of the University of Miami, Clare King at Johns Hopkins University, Rajesh Kumar of the Aarhus School of Business in Denmark, Liz Lorant at the Open Society Institute, Michael Moffitt of the University of Oregon School of Law, Michele Williams of MIT Sloan, and Craig Zelizer of the Alliance for Conflict Transformation. Mopsy Kennedy helped brainstorm titles for the book. Tim Gearan provided Monday-night music during which parts of this book were written. An anonymous client of Lobel, Novins, & Lamont helped support our work in the hope that it may contribute to the peaceful resolution of disputes.

We are particularly indebted to Jamil Mahuad, former president of Ecuador, for contributing the final chapter of this book.

Shannon Quinn, a former editor of the *Negotiation Journal* and indispensable editor of this book, worked closely with us to refine the text and smooth the language. Her guidance and book development may have translated into more work for the authors, but we trust less for the reader. Our editors at Viking Penguin marked up nearly every page in order to make this text easier to read. Rick Kot, Jane von Mehren, and Alessandra Lusardi brought their keen minds and careful edits to our book. It's been a pleasure to work with them. And our agents—Andrew Wylie and Sarah Chalfant—kept us in good hands so we could focus on writing this book.

We feel blessed by the support of our families who joined us in spirit and enthusiasm on this book-writing journey. Elizabeth Sealey brought her business expertise to bear. Susan Dole shared in her knowledge of labor-management disputes. And Susan and Ron Shapiro read draft after draft, offered feedback, and remain two of the most dedicated and loving parents a person could ever know.

No acknowledgment can do justice to the debt we owe to our wives, Carrie Fisher and Mia Shapiro. Writing a practical book about emotions is not just an intellectual exercise. It is a lived experience. As we developed prescriptive ideas, we often tried them out when negotiating with our spouses. We learned a lot and are grateful for their patience and support.

—Roger and Dan
Cambridge, Massachusetts

Analytical
Table of Contents

Getting to Yes

Roger Fisher, William Ury and Bruce Patton

With over 2 million copies sold in over 20 different languages, *Getting to Yes* is the most successful negotiation book on the market!

Negotiating is a way of life for the majority of us. Whether we're at work, at home or simply going out, we want to participate in the decisions that affect us. Nowadays, hardly anyone gets through the day without a single negotiation, yet, few of us are armed with the effective, powerful negotiating skills that prevent stubborn haggling and ensure mutual problem-solving.

This book cuts through the jargon to present a few easily remembered principles that will guide you to success, no matter what the other side does or whatever dirty tricks they resort to.

Contents include:
– Don't bargain over positions
– Separate people from the problem
– Insist on objective criteria
– What if they won't play?

Getting to Yes has sold over two million copies worldwide in over 20 different languages and over 170,000 copies in the UK, making it the bestselling book on negotiation on the market. The book is recognized worldwide as the most effective and practical guide to negotiation and has helped millions of people secure win-win outcomes in constructive negotiations.

ROGER FISHER is Williston Professor of Law Emeritus at Harvard Law School and Director of the Harvard Negotiation Project.

WILLIAM URY is an internationally known specialist in negotiation and associate director of the Programme on Negotiation at Harvard Law School.

BRUCE PATTON is deputy director of the Harvard Negotiation Project.

BUSINESS
BOOKS

**Order more Harvard Negotiation Project titles
from your local bookshop, or have them delivered
direct to your door by Bookpost**

☐ **Getting to Yes** Roger Fisher,
William Ury, Bruce Patton   9781844131464   £8.99

Free post and packing
Overseas customers allow £2 per paperback

Phone: 01624 677237

Post: Random House Books
c/o Bookpost, PO Box 29, Douglas, Isle of Man IM99 1BQ

Fax: 01624 670923

email: bookshop@enterprise.net

Cheques (payable to Bookpost) and credit cards accepted

Prices and availability subject to change without notice.
Allow 28 days for delivery.
When placing your order, please state if you do not wish to receive any
additional information.

www.randomhouse.co.uk

BUSINESS
BOOKS